For a Time Like This

Michael Jelliffe

For a Time Like This

For a Time Like This
by Michael Jelliffe

Copyright © 2024 Michael A. Jelliffe
All rights reserved

In accordance with copyright laws, this book or parts thereof may not be reproduced in any form, stored in an retrieval system, or transmitted in any form by any means - electronic, mechanical, photocopy, recording, or otherwise - without prior written permission of the publisher.

No AI Training: Without in any way limiting the author's exclusive rights under copyright, any use of this publication to "train" generative artificial intelligence (AI) technologies to generate text is expressly prohibited. The author reserves all rights to license uses of this work for generative AI training and development of machine learning language models.

Published by Nenge Books, Australia, 2024
ABN 26809396184
nengebooks1@gmail.com
www.nengebooks.com

Design and desktop by Nenge Books
Photos copyright © 2024 Michael A. Jelliffe, apart from:
photo of mumu on page 76, copyright © 2024 David Metcalfe;
photos on page 6 & 23 © 2005 Merv Moffatt
photos on page 97 & top two page 99 © 2006 Ed Laninga
photo page 89 courtesy Dean Johnston
For some photos I have been unable to trace the original photographer but used them as they have been given to me in the course of MAF work.
Watercolour paintings from originals © 2024 Michael A. Jelliffe

Cover photo - Elders honour Mike & Kathy Jelliffe, greeting them in traditional dress after they flew in to Erave airstrip for a weekend of church training ministry.

Nenge Books provides publishing services to independent authors using print-on-demand technology for hard copy books, and ebooks.

ISBN 978-0-6459597-6-5

Dedication

Dedicated to my wife, Kathy, and my three children, Kylie, Tim and Cameron, for their support for me during this period of time, and to my friends and colleagues who shared these three years of my life with me.

On Eagles' Wings

To reach up high above the trees
has been man's dream for many years;
on eagles' wings to bring good news
and cross those barriers of leaves
and wood, and time and space;
and reach, in time, that last hidden race
who, locked in history's dark past,
wait for a Saviour to come at last,
and free them from the grip of death;
to know God's love and power - life's breath.

copyright © 1987 Michael Jelliffe

Contents

FOREWORD	ix
PREFACE	xi
1. A DAY TO REMEMBER	1
2. DISCERNING DISCIPLESHIP	8
3. SEEKING SERVANT LEADERSHIP	11
4. P2-MFQ	14
5. THE AFTERMATH	19
6. THE IMPACT ON THE MIN COMMUNITY	24
7. PILOT DEBRIEFING	32
8. HIJACK THREATS	36
9. AIRCRAFT IN, AIRCRAFT OUT	42
10. PRACTICAL RESPONSES TO SPIRITUAL THREATS	47
11. RESPONDING TO THE MIN COMMUNITY	54
12. RECRUITMENT, HIV & BIRD FLU	62
13. ENGAGING IN THE WIDER COMMUNITY	71
14. WHEN TRUST IS BROKEN	77
15. MISSIONARY CHALLENGES	81
16. P2-MFJ	91
17. P2-MFO and P2-MFP	100

18. WORN OUT	107
19. FLIGHT TRAINING SCHOOL	115
20. PROVINCIAL CHALLENGES	119
.21. NEW OPPORTUNITIES	130
22. FLIGHT CO-ORDINATION	134
23. ELECTION TIME STRATEGIES	136
24. ADVISING GOVERNMENT	140
25. ORO FLOOD EMERGENCY	146
26. GUNSHOTS	151
27. CAA CONTACT	154
28. COMPENSATION THREATS	155
29. BREAKDOWN	159
EPILOGUE	163
POSTSCRIPT	165

FOREWORD

The idiom, "Don't judge a person until you have walked a mile in their shoes," conveys to us that we cannot truly understand someone else's reality unless we have lived their experience. At face value, one may conclude that leading a modern mission organisation made up of highly motivated and well trained aviation professionals, strongly committed to improving the lives of isolated people, could be nothing less than straightforward!

In *For a Time Like This*, Mike Jelliffe gives us some glimpses into the enigmatic and somewhat mysterious challenges of leading a mission team utilising small aircraft in a hostile aviation environment to bring help, hope and healing to isolated communities. Mike's detailed recollections of his time as General Manager for Mission Aviation Fellowship in Papua New Guinea, and his craft with words, gives the reader graphic revelation of challenges few people ever face in life.

During the relatively recent COVID-19 pandemic, the word 'pivot' became increasingly used in the English language, conveying the changes that individuals and organisations needed to make during a time of much societal upheaval. During those days, one's ability to pivot in a timely manner became make or break for businesses and organisations. Well before the time of the COVID-19 pandemic, Mike was practicing the art of 'pivoting' as he led MAF through some incredibly challenging times in PNG.

I have known Mike now for a couple of decades and at times worked closely alongside him within MAF. I consider him a courageous leader, forward-looking and holistic in his consideration for how management decisions will impact the lives of staff he is leading and those who benefit from MAFs service. I know him to be a curious person, reading and studying widely, exploring, seeking greater understanding so that he can improve the organisation through his leadership.

As you read this book, in which Mike so effectively paints pictures with his words, you will not only be entertained with interesting stories, but also appreciate some of the joys, privileges and challenges faced by mission leaders. Above all I hope that, like Mike, you chose to live faithfully for Jesus Christ, who promised to be with his followers "always"[1] and who declared (to a much earlier Christian leader - the Apostle Paul), that his "grace to be sufficient and his power made perfect in weaknesses"[2]. I know this is Mike's testimony, I want it to be mine, and I trust it becomes yours too!

Stephen Charlesworth
Director, Strategic Development
MAF International
October 2024

---

1. Matthew 28:20
2. 2 Corinthians 12:9

PREFACE

Mission Aviation Fellowship (MAF) first came to my attention when, as a fresh 19 year old university drop out in 1971, I visited Papua New Guinea (PNG) to spend a few weeks volunteering with a project building a Teacher's College at Dauli, near Tari, in the Southern Highlands Province. The project was partly Rotary sponsored and my father and mother had visited the previous year as part of my father's role coordinating Rotary Australia's involvement. The other main partner was Asia Pacific Christian Mission (APCM), an interdenominational mission which had been pioneering with church, health and educational initiatives in many parts of the Southern Highlands and Western Province since first contact with the tribes who lived there.

While staying with missionaries at Dauli, I was tasked with driving their Land Rover the 40-minute trip on dirt bush roads into Tari airstrip to meet MAF flights, and return with whatever people, mail or goods were destined for Dauli. The little yellow Cessna 185's or 206's would somehow have found their way around the mountains and under the clouds from Wewak, Mt Hagen or Port Moresby, or numerous bush airstrips in between. We'd hear the drone of the engine long before seeing the plane, which we'd watch as it touched down and taxied into the parking area.

I'd had a couple of lessons learning to fly previously and getting airborne in a light aircraft was not a new experience.

My doctor father was also a pilot and built a 2-seater aircraft (Jodel D-11) in which we had done a number of trips together. But I had never seen aviation at this level before, bush flying at its best. I'd previously imagined the only scope for a career was as an airline pilot.

Soon after, I was offered work with a commercial airline operating light aircraft extensively around PNG as a Traffic Officer, based in Mt Hagen. Thus began what became a lifelong career in aviation.

Something else happened while I was at Dauli. The calibre of the missionaries' lives and the growing recognition that I needed to make some changes in my life, changes that only God could facilitate, led me to commit myself to following Jesus Christ. So my journey in aviation came hand in hand with my journey of discovery of spiritual life in Christ. It was not long before my career goal became the desire to work for God in Christian mission aviation.

As I chatted with the MAF pilots at Tari and then watched spellbound as their little yellow airplanes disappeared behind the clouds, I would never in my wildest dreams have imagined that one day I would not only fly with MAF, but 30 years later become the PNG field leader of the mission.

This then is the story of my three years as General Manager of MAF PNG, February 2005 – December 2007. Some may not agree with some of my recollections, and some may dispute them. We all see events through our own perspective in context and time. Be that as it may, this is my recollections of that period of time in my life, some of the events that happened and my response to them. Obviously it is only a selection of events but ones that were most significant for me and the operation. At the same time, I hope I am able to convey the reality of life as it was, and in a way which honours the amazing missionaries and nationals who I had the privilege to work with, and who have given their all in serving Christ.

Much of it is dealing with very practical issues and not always very spiritual, but unmanageable unless one appreciates the spiritual nature of the world at large, and Christian ministry in particular. That is the context of management.

The challenges were huge, and the price paid in service for Christ can be extreme, whether in an emotional, mental or physical sense, or in life itself. But without the willingness of Christ's disciples to lay down all and go to the hard places, the gospel will not be advanced. The growth of the church in Papua New Guinea is testimony to that.

The events I talk about in this book are generally in chronological order, some specific dates are mentioned, but some events are lumped together to maintain the theme. It is only possible to mention a few of the extraordinary things that happened but all occurred within the context of 'normal' day to day flying operations and aviation business. Of course, most people would regard even normal operations of a bush airline in PNG as extraordinary! But in reality, they became normal for us.

I have left many characters nameless, used first names for others who played a more significant role in the events and full names where that is necessary in the context, recognising there are many who should be included and are not. If I am seen to cause offence or misrepresent the truth at all in anything I have written, I offer my sincere apology and stand to be corrected.

Michael Jelliffe
October 2024

1. A DAY TO REMEMBER

My suspicions about Giri (not his real name) were raised before actually meeting him face to face. He'd called me a week or two earlier and, with glowing and to my mind somewhat artificial zeal, congratulated me on being appointed as General Manager for Mission Aviation Fellowship's Papua New Guinea operation. In fact, he had gone as far as sending his generous congratulations, in person, across the airwaves of a local radio station. I couldn't help but think that his intent was to impress me more than his listeners.

"Have you listened in and heard?" he enquired over the phone, eager that I receive his overflowing exuberance.

As it turned out, I had not. He, however, had heard about our Commissioning Service and did not miss attending.

It was February 12th, 2005. A day to remember.

The MAF hangar at Mt Hagen's Kagamuga airport, headquarters of MAF's operation in the centre of PNG's highlands, had been cleared of aircraft and decked out with chairs. Missionary staff, mainly pilots and engineers and their families from the nine bases around the country, had gathered with many of our Papua New Guinean staff for the occasion. In typical Melanesian style, *leis* (flower or decorative necklaces) in different colours were ceremoniously placed over the heads of visitors and dignitaries, including my wife Kathy and myself, by our female PNG staff members.

Speeches were made by Board members and senior MAF leaders. The retiring General Manager, Mark Emerson, and MAF Australia/NZ CEO, Bill Harding, made a solemn presentation to me of the items of most importance in the job – an axe, to fight my way out of the office; a pile of files almost too high to carry; and a can of Mortein spray, to keep any pests away! A group of local pastors, whom we had invited to represent the churches in Mt Hagen, formed a ring around Kathy and myself as we knelt on cushions. With hands laid on our head or shoulders, or hands outstretched towards us, they commissioned us in prayer to serve God in this role.

The service was significant in signalling the start of a new regime, and we were glad to have this endorsement and support. In Melanesia ceremony is important, and leaders, 'big men', are respected. MAF exists to serve missions and churches in remote areas as a primary ministry, and to be commissioned by these Papua New Guinean pastors and Board members was fitting. In fact, some commented that it had never been done like this before.

"It is a great privilege to take on the role of General Manager," I reflected as I spoke to those gathered. "Yes, there will be many decisions about finances, housing, aircraft, people, but the measure of my success as GM is not in terms of dollars and cents at the end of the year. It is in terms of the value that I have been extending the Kingdom of God in your hearts and minds, and the extent to which we as a mission community have added Kingdom value to every aviation activity we have carried out.

"I have a vision of MAF PNG not as a fleet of aircraft, but as a group of people who are touching those around them with God's grace and love:

"So that every staff member gets home at night and says, I am so thankful for my workmates because God has blessed me through them today.

"So that every passenger gets off the aircraft saying I've been drawn closer to God because of these MAF people.

"So that every person who comes to the ticket counter goes away saying, these people care about my travel, they were so helpful and God has touched me through them.

"So that the government agencies we work with say, these MAF people are so committed to their mission and God that we love to work with them because of their gift of service.

"Aviation is our business, but this is our mission - to be agents of God's grace as we use the grace gifts God has given us."

The service concluded with cutting a cake, complete with an airstrip and aircraft as decorations, and refreshments for all. The hangar was full of people and so it was no surprise that I didn't notice a new face among the visitors. I never did find out how Giri had managed to join the hangar crowd of otherwise invited guests that day.

Kathy and I returned to Papua New Guinea in mid 2004 after thirteen years absence from the country. Our previous sojourn in PNG spanning twenty years had included over a decade as a pilot in MAF, when we were fortunate to be based in several locations stretching across the far reaches of its provinces. I flew back into Tari frequently. This was combined with several years previously in commercial aviation and as an urban missionary pastor/trainer with Asia Pacific Christian Mission (APCM) in Port Moresby. Mid-career study at

Fuller Theological Seminary, School of World Mission, gave academic and intellectual value to our experience. As a result, we were able to gain a good understanding of the people and the country of PNG, and a deep appreciation and love for both, while missiological considerations in this cross-cultural ministry were prominent.

Within a few months of our return to MAF and PNG in mid 2004, while preparing to take up a role as a pilot once again, I was asked to consider a change - to take on the position of General Manager. I felt unprepared to make the change and inadequate for the role. In fact, when making enquiries earlier with MAF about returning to PNG, I had been asked if I wanted to work in management or fly. I chose flying and had taken six months off work to gain my Airline Transport Pilot Licence, a requirement MAF stipulated at that time for Twin Otter pilots. With this latest request I could see my hands slipping off the control column - and didn't like it!

But through the encouragement of the trusted people we sought counsel from, and the daily positive inspiration which came through reading the Scriptures, we understood that this was in fact an invitation from the Lord Himself. Passages from Ezekiel were particularly poignant, such as chapter 33, where God commissions Ezekiel to be a watchman over the house of Israel, warning people of their evil ways and the need to turn back to God. There was a sense in which this appointment was as a watchman over the ministry of MAF in PNG, warning of the need to recognise evil intentions and maintain a focus on God through Christ.

We looked back and recognised that while we felt insecure in taking on such a role, our years of ministry experience both in and out of MAF, our time in Papua New Guinea, and our various life and work experiences since, had all been part of

God's preparation. As one person very close to us said, *"you were meant for a time like this"*, quoting the Old Testament Esther's experience. These words would become so significant for me later.

On several occasions in the first few weeks of our arrival back in Papua New Guinea, our interaction with Papua New Guinean acquaintances made us clearly aware that it was their prayers that had paved the way for our return. While passing through Port Moresby enroute to Mt Hagen we attended a prayer meeting of local church friends, who commented that they had prayed for us regularly during the past thirteen years of our absence. We were humbled to consider that it was our friends here whose Macedonian call had brought us back. We had returned to be among our friends, to serve with them and to serve them. Our own agendas were secondary to theirs. How could that be demonstrated better than by being commissioned by our Papua New Guinean friends. It also shaped how we would approach this leadership ministry.

Twin Otter (DHC6) endorsement training prior to GM appointment.

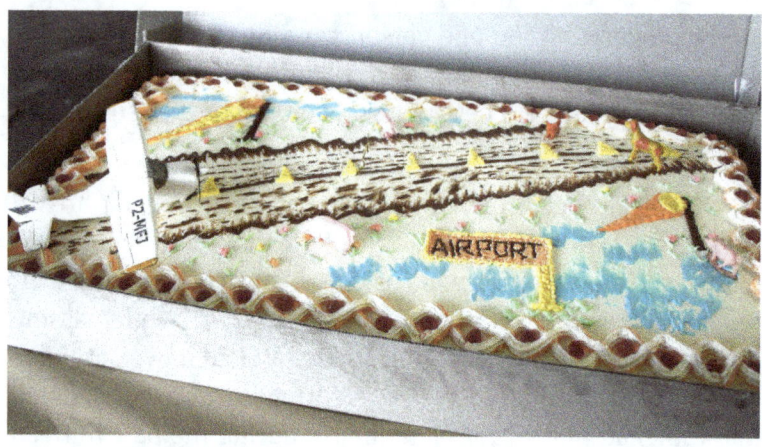

Commissioning cake (note the aircraft registration - MFJ : Mike Foxtrot Jelliffe?).

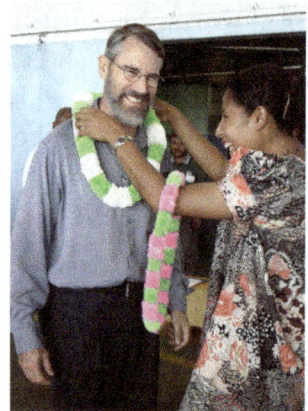

Receiving a lei from Sarah.

MAF PNG Board members and local pastors pray for us.

Kagamuga airport - Mt Hagen township is 14km away.

2. DISCERNING DISCIPLESHIP

Giri had called to make an appointment to see me and offer first-hand congratulations. He wished to present me with a token gift as well, an item made many years ago apparently by his father, a pastor in a remote area. As he introduced himself and we shook hands, I sensed that my initial reservations were not unfounded. I noticed that the last joint on his left-hand little finger was missing, and there were tattoo marks on his hands. He never produced the gift.

He was a young man made older by his lifestyle, that of a *raskal*, the popular local term for a troublemaker and criminal. The towns in Papua New Guinea have become known for their rascal gangs, both responsible and feared for crime at all levels. Urbanisation in PNG has been rapid, with infrastructure and employment opportunities sadly severely lacking. The rise of the rascal gang element, often with codes of behaviour emulating the strict rural village codes which include brutal rites of passage and initiation, has been an urban response.

In earlier years in PNG, from 1987 to 1991, we had worked in discipleship and related ministries with a group of young men and women in Port Moresby. A number of these were from *raskal* backgrounds, including one young man who had spent time in prison for bashing a white person! He had become a faithful and trusted friend, appreciative of Kathy's work in teaching him basic reading and writing skills. So Giri posed no threat to me. Rather I saw him as another young man with a troubled past hopefully seeking a positive future.

It was obvious that Giri had been a regular user of *buai*, betel nut, which when mixed with lime and mustard plant not only induces an intoxicating affect for the chewer, but also fills the mouth with red stain. The cracks between his teeth and his gums displayed the tell-tale red. Some churches do not endorse the use of buai and MAF did not encourage it because of its propensity to cause cancers in the mouth and affect one's senses.

His clothes were dirty and in general terms he was unkempt, though no more than many young people from the squatter settlements. But he had brought along a reference and passed the paper to me to verify personally. It was his HIV test, apparently negative. With great sincerity he explained to me how he had, in the last week, decided to follow the Lord, and the fact that he was no longer chewing *buai* was a good indication.

Even more spectacular though was his claim to have been healed of AIDS. The test report confirmed this, he claimed. His 'wife' had come with him on this visit to me at the MAF HQ, though she remained at a distance from the building. While Giri's HIV report was no doubt good news for her, she was in fact also another man's wife.

True discipleship is a genuine following of Jesus Christ, who takes us as we are and leads us to be where He wants us to be. In my years of dealing with people from all walks of life I have learned never to be surprised at people's situations, or to judge them by their appearances. At the start of that journey we all carry with us baggage that we will discard. How much of that baggage is essential to discard before making the journey is difficult to judge, but my feeling was that I wanted to see Giri shed a little more baggage before I would be sure of his genuineness.

I suggested he attend the local church of his denomination, which happened to be the same church we attended, and seek assistance from leaders of the church to encourage his discipleship journey. I sensed I would not be surprised to see him there one Sunday soon.

Street boys playing dart games, Mt Hagen.

PMV travel, Mt Hagen.

3. SEEKING SERVANT LEADERSHIP

My first week was spent getting myself generally acquainted with the office and staff, including some visits to other bases in other towns, and conducting some handover meetings with the previous General Manager before he flew out. It seemed like a whirlwind introduction!

During our time of service in MAF so far we had seen at least five General Managers come and go, all different in their personality and approach. One of the values which I wanted to foster was a positive relationship of trust with the team, missionaries and PNG staff, rather than establish a hierarchy of power.

Hierarchy should not be confused with authority. From earlier experiences in an organisation with a very flat structure, I determined that in any future leadership role I would seek to exercise the authority inherent in the role but seek to do so in a manner which did not promote hierarchy, the 'them and us' syndrome that undermines relationships in so many organisations.

So I initiated some rearrangement of the HQ offices. By swapping the GM office to an adjacent room, I could enlarge the space to allow not only a desk but also have room to install a couch and chairs with a coffee table. We found a second-hand couch and two lounge chairs and a coffee table in storage, and I was able to fulfil what I considered one of the most important visual aspects of my role. To sit behind a big desk and communicate with people reinforces hierarchy and position and can easily be intimidating for staff. So, I made it a point that I would always try to sit on the lounge chairs with people who came to see me, at the same physical level, unless the nature of the meeting preferred being at my desk.

I wanted the nature of my leadership to be seen as relational rather than just organisational. Authority can be gained in two ways. Designated or positional authority is gained with the appointment to a position of authority within the organisation, and works through rules and structures. Things like uniforms, fancy office furniture, privilege and executive vehicles tend to reinforce it. Relational authority is earned and works through trust and respect. I had been given the positional authority but I wanted the mutual trust and respect of those I was responsible for, the relational base, to be firm if my leadership was to be successful.

Time Magazine some years ago published a story about Nelson Mandela, asking him about his leadership style. He replied that he learned leadership when he was a small boy growing up in his African village herding cattle. He would walk behind the cattle with a small stick and if one of them started to stray, he would give it a light prod on the back with the stick. That was his model of leadership.

Leadership does not always mean you have to be out the front. Effective leaders are able to guide their team in the direction needed. That is best achieved through relationships that encourage and positively influence rather than rules that demand obedience. It seems to be a shame when leaders have to resort to demanding obedience to rules to get co-operation – following the letter of the law but not the spirit of it.

When the MAF PNG Leadership Team had been approached with the proposal to appoint me into the General Manager role, they agreed, with the wise proviso that other executive support staff, including an Executive Officer, also be recruited to assist me. At that time there was no Human Resources person to deal with international staff issues and no Ground Operations Manager or Training Manager. The mission was under-resourced in terms of its senior management staffing, with a focus on aviation, not management related expertise, in recruiting.

It is one of the great challenges for volunteer mission organisations. Recruitment is dependent on people responding to the challenge, in this case, world mission. It is not always a matter of hiring staff who have suitable qualifications and experience; it is more a matter of assessing where those who volunteer will fit. I hoped we would see more focused recruitment on management positions in future.

Joining the cultural celebrations at Siassi, Morobe Province.

4. P2-MFQ

At 1:30 pm on Tuesday 22nd February 2005, ten days after my commissioning, I had just sat down in my new General Manager's office after a week and a half of hectic handover from my predecessor. The Finance Manager, Patrick, was about to initiate me into the mysteries of the organisation's finances. As we both sat on the lounge chairs, I had actually opened to page one of my folder. With a knock on the door, another senior staffer urgently advised that an aircraft, a Twin Otter, P2-MFQ was missing, reportedly crashed.

In a close-knit mission aviation community, these are the words we never want to hear. While flying in Papua New Guinea is not unsafe, the combination of weather, mountains and airstrips carved out of the jungle, provide an environment which is unforgiving and unrelenting. The reputation of the country in aviation is unfortunately one that is shrouded in a history of accidents which have claimed the lives of pilots and passengers regardless of their organisation. MAF PNG's legacy at that stage included eight pilot fatalities since operations commenced 54 years ago. Most were known to me; several were close colleagues.

A multitude of thoughts raced through my mind.

Is this real?

Is this possible?

Has the crash been confirmed?

Who are the pilots?

What do I now have to do as field leader of this mission?

How do we organise for a rescue effort?

How do we provide support for the families?

At the same time, there was that horrible sinking feeling in my gut that hopes for the best against all the odds, but expects the worst.

Fortunately one of the jobs I had done while assisting the Chief Pilot in the months prior to this was to review and type up a flow chart for use in such emergencies. Little did I realise how valuable this would be so soon. The first minutes are a blur, but a team of senior leaders was assembled and vital actions commenced. When we reviewed the events later in retrospect, we marvelled at the unity of purpose and action that had followed, something only possible when Someone greater than ourselves was involved.

As we gained more information from first responders on the HF radio, the story emerged. The aircraft had been attempting to land at Wobagen airstrip, located in a steep sided valley in the country's remote Sandaun (West Sepik) province, about halfway between Tari and Telefomin. This airstrip had only recently been opened after months of delay by civil aviation authorities. The airstrip was partly covered in a low fog preventing a landing, even though the rest of the valley was clear.

On the other side of a small ridge-line in the centre of the valley was the old Bimin airstrip, part of which had subsided in a landslip, rendering it unserviceable as an airstrip. The new airstrip at Wobagen had only recently been opened up as an alternative in the valley. Local people, including a pastor, had watched the aircraft from the old Bimin airstrip as the pilots circled around the valley, attempting to land by approaching their final approach lower than normal to get under the fog.

As they watched, the aircraft was seen to fly low along the valley, clip trees and plunge into thick jungle undergrowth. Within little over an hour a runner had crossed the valley with a report, sent now by HF radio. The two pilots, Chris Hansen and Richard West, had reportedly been killed. The passengers had all escaped virtually unharmed. Our confusion was mixed with horror and sadness.

Already our rescue efforts had focused on getting a doctor to the scene as soon as possible. One of the miracles of that day was that in this highland's location, which is renowned for its bad weather, the whole afternoon remained clear, and no rescue aircraft movements were hampered. While a giant mine operator in the province, Ok Tedi Mining Ltd, despatched a rescue helicopter to the scene from Tabubil, we despatched one of our own aircraft (a Cessna 206) to pick up a mission doctor at Rumginae. He would need to go to Agali, the nearest airstrip to Wobagen, about 10 minutes flight time away, ready to then fly into Wobagen by helicopter. A second aircraft (a Twin Otter) was despatched to pick up survivors, who were helicoptered to Agali, to then be flown to the hospital at the mining town of Tabubil, about 30 minutes flight away.

The two pilots were based with their families at the isolated MAF base at Telefomin, in the westernmost highlands of PNG. Their wives, Janice Hansen and Cherie West, obviously deeply distressed, had been informed of the accident and awaited news near the base HF radio, the only method of communication with the outside world. It meant they heard all the reports of the rescue efforts as they happened. While the reports coming from the pastor on the radio at Bimin indicated the pilots had died, we needed to have positive identification before releasing a statement and confirming this to the families.

When this identification came from the mission doctor now at Agali, who knew both pilots personally, I recall a deep anguish, recognising that it was my responsibility to speak to the wives on the radio and confirm this to them. It was the hardest moment of my career. I recall just trying to say as simply as I could that we can confirm they have died. I also remember thinking very clearly that I never, ever, wanted to have to do that again.

One of the events which had been an emotional landmark in my own life was the death of pilot Paul Summerfield in 1985. Paul and I flew together in our MAF orientation program in 1977 at Ballarat in Victoria, Australia, and were co-workers in MAF PNG. His death in PNG flying a Cessna TU206 aircraft which I had also flown many hours in, affected me profoundly, and changed the way I looked on life. His funeral had unlocked something emotionally in me, the tears which seemed to flow unashamedly and without reserve had expressed deep sorrow, while releasing a desire to love people in a way I had held back from before. So I was not a newcomer to this anguish, yet recognised that for the wives this would be far, far greater than mine could ever be.

Recognising our need to support the Hansen and West families immediately, we despatched our other Twin Otter out from Mt Hagen to Telefomin, a one-hour trip west, with two MAF families who could offer their love and pastoral support. I recall feeling that this was a primary role that I should take, but as I discussed this with the Emergency Response team, we felt it better that I stay in Mt Hagen, coordinate the response effort and maintain effective communication at all levels. Mt Hagen had full communications around PNG and the world, Telefomin at that stage did not.

Soon after the rescue helicopter reached Bimin, which was nearer the accident site, at about 3:30pm, we received word that the passengers had walked up from the crash site to Bimin airstrip. The bodies of the pilots had also been carried out on bush stretchers. A couple of passengers were attended to by the rescue helicopter paramedic for minor injuries, and the pilot's bodies flown to the Agali airstrip nearby where the mission doctor was waiting. We never received a bill for these helicopter services, such is the level of support for each other that aviation organisations in PNG enjoy and appreciate.

By dusk on what was an agonising yet remarkable day, the rescue aircraft crews were all safely back at their base; the passengers who may have had possible non-visible injuries had been flown to Tabubil Hospital; the pilots' bodies were in the morgue at Tabubil; and a pastoral care team was in Telefomin with the pilots' families.

The aircraft had been found, rescue and medical teams taken to the site, and a successful follow up carried out in just a few afternoon hours in what must be one of the most inhospitable and remotest areas of Papua New Guinea. With communications limited to HF and VHF aircraft radio, a team of people committed to each other's welfare and working together in harmony, together with the oversight of a loving God, we marvelled at what was able to be accomplished in such a short time. It was a trial by fire for me though. At no stage over the next weeks and months did I feel that I really understood what was happening or have confidence in my abilities to navigate the team and ministry through it.

As we learned more of the accident though, it only heightened the reality of the spiritual nature of MAF's ministry, and our unanswered questions.

5. THE AFTERMATH

The next day a team with some engineers was sent to Wobagen to begin an investigation of the accident. We grounded all flights except to allow our MAF missionary staff from all around the country to fly to Mt Hagen, where families were billeted by the Hagen families. I think Kathy and I were the only ones on the team who had experienced an accident like this before. I believed that it was essential that we grieve together as a mission family and work out where we go from here together in fellowship.

Some of my reasoning was based on our own experience when MAF pilot Jim Johnston died in an aircraft accident in 1979 in the Sepik province in the north of PNG. We were based in Kawito to the south and due to poor communication networks, only HF radio, had been very limited in what we knew was going in during the search and eventual location of the aircraft in a mountain range. Once a memorial service had been arranged, bad weather prevented Kathy and I from flying in and joining the rest of the MAF PNG families (there was no other transport option than flying). While we understood the mechanics of bad weather as a valid reason to miss out, we did feel disappointed and isolated from what the rest of the mission family was experiencing, with no opportunity to share in that grief. It was a very different experience in 1985 with Paul Summerfield's situation, which as I have said, was catalytic for me in dealing with grief.

The reports that came back from the accident site were by nature graphic. How could anyone have survived this?

The front of the aircraft which took the full force was so badly damaged, there was little hope of the pilots surviving. But the cabin area behind the cockpit was intact. The Cabin Attendant hit his head and suffered some concussion. A woman was holding a baby throughout the event. The forward section of the cabin contained bulk items of cargo and baggage, securely tied down under a specialised restraining net. They had not moved.

The passengers were able to open their rear cabin door and exit the aircraft. There was no fire, as is common in aircraft accidents. Yet another miracle surfaced. The country is limestone country dotted with sink-holes, a metre or less up to several metres wide, and who knows how deep? A tree which had been downed by the aircraft now sat reaching from the cabin door outwards to the other side of a sink-hole. The passengers walked to safety across this log, otherwise they may well have stepped out and fallen into the sink-hole.

We began to recognise that in the midst of utmost tragedy for some, there was also miraculous intervention for others. Accepting both was so difficult.

The care team stayed in Telefomin for a day or two before coming into Mt Hagen with the two pilot families. A couple of months earlier Chris Hansen had been one of the instructors for a Twin Otter (DHC6) conversion course I attended in preparation to return to flying. Cherie West and their children had stayed with us at one stage while in transit through Mt Hagen as well. I had fun memories of waking up one morning to find their youngest son, about 4 years old, standing next to our bed staring at my face from a few centimetres away! The bonds of friendship are far deeper than just workmates. There is a fellowship of love when you are living and working side by side in a mission environment like this.

As the Twin Otter returning from Telefomin with the pilots' families pulled up outside our airport terminal in Mt Hagen, I felt at a loss to know what to do. Many of our Mt Hagen team had gathered at the terminal. Instinctively I walked forward to greet them as they stepped off the aircraft, thankful that the care team were with them too. Others came forward with me and quickly surrounded the incoming families in the fellowship of grief.

It took me back to Paul Summerfield's accident nearly 20 years earlier, and his wife Sally's situation with her four small children. On the day of his funeral in Mt Hagen, I had flown MAF's Cessna 402C from Port Moresby with Paul's father travelling in the co-pilot's seat. Soon after we took off, we noticed that there was a rainbow visible in front of us, 360 degrees wrapped around the nose of the aircraft. We couldn't see any moisture but we must have flown through a very light mist, unusual on a fine, clear morning! Some things can't be explained scientifically though!

"It's a sign of God's presence with us," remarked Paul's father to me. In all my years of flying I had seen the 'pilot's halo' many times as it cast its shadow on a cloud layer just below the aircraft, the aircraft shadow as a cross circled by a rainbow. But I had never seen it around the aircraft like this, nor have I again to this day.

Later on as I shared this with others, I discovered that Sally also, departing Madang for Mt Hagen in MAF's Beechcraft Baron, apparently saw the same effect. The miraculous in the midst of tragedy. The reminder that God does not desert us in the worst times. In fact we may be more likely to be aware of God's presence in those times.

I wondered if these families had seen evidence of this on their flight in?

Over the next couple of weeks Kathy and I had a number of opportunities to spend time with both Janice and Cherie in the immediate aftermath of the accident. Counselling people who are bereaved was not in our list of academic credits nor something we had any real experience in. But I am so thankful that God opened up the opportunity for us to contribute to their planning for the future in a considerate and pastoral way.

In fact, one of the highlights for us some months later was to receive a card from Janice, thanking us for our ministry at the time, with the comment, *"You were meant for a time like this,"* quoting from the book of Esther. A missionary doctor acquaintance had also sent us a card, saying "I'm confident that the Lord has prepared you to be where you are *for a time such as this*". It has been one of the most poignant reminders to me that God had appointed me to this role despite my reservations and reluctance... kicking and screaming may be more truthful!

Within a few days, various members of both Chris, Janice, Richard and Cherie's families began to arrive from NZ and Australia and joined in to provide the support that only family can give. This provided another opportunity to witness some amazing aspects of this tragic event.

At 10.30am on Saturday 26th February, we joined the families and MAF staff for a Memorial Service for Richard and Chris in the Mt Hagen Baptist Church.

As we gathered round their wives and children in prayer, it touched our hearts to have Dean Johnston join us. Dean was a small boy when his father, Jim, was the pilot who died in the aircraft accident in 1979 while we were at Kawito. Now one of our MAF PNG pilots himself, Dean provided a measure of comfort especially for the children. Perhaps it also helped me draw some closure on his father's death?

Memorial Service for Chris and Richard.

Joining in prayer for the pilots' families (Dean on right).

6. THE IMPACT ON THE MIN COMMUNITY

None of this happened in a vacuum, in fact there is an incredible depth of history behind these events. This was the fourth major MAF accident on Min soil (the local Telefomin peoples are the Min tribe) and now brought the number of pilot fatalities on their land to five. It was a statistic which struck hard for the Min community.

One of the very early MAF pilots flying in the Telefomin area, John Harverson, disappeared in June 1967 while on a flight between Telefomin and Olsobip. The flight crosses the majestic Hindenburg Wall, a towering almost vertical cliff face thousands of feet high and stretching over 80 km, which attracts the build-up of cloud storms very quickly. While every now and then local people trekking through the high mountain country in the area will report seeing something that looks like part of an aircraft, no wreckage has ever been found. Over the next few years two other pilots died tragically in aircraft accidents, Bob Peaker at Eliptamin and Roy Hoey at Selbang. No one felt the grief of losing two more pilots than the Min community at large.

Our own personal experience of Telefomin came in 1981 when we were assigned to the MAF base there after the previous pilot family, who were the first ones permanently assigned to the base, had to leave for medical reasons. We enjoyed a year and a half of flying around the Min community airstrips with a Cessna 206 with 310HP turbo charged engine and fitted with a Robertson STOL kit[1]. Apart from the majestic mountain flying in the area, the highlight for us though was getting to know people in the community at large. Needless to say, I was still familiar with Telefomin and the surrounding airstrip communities from subsequent more recent flights to the area, though it had been over 20 years since we had lived there.

The Min airstrip communities wished to pay their respects to honour the pilots and their families and so a tour with families was planned to take them to several airstrips to participate in a memorial event at each. A Twin Otter was allocated to do the tour around the airstrip communities in the Telefomin area most impacted. As General Manager, I joined the families for this tour. Two of these community encounters are lodged very clearly in my memory.

The first was at Wobegon, the site of the accident and our first port of call. Once on the ground we could see across the valley to blue tarpaulins and a clearing in the trees where the crash site was. All the people from the Wobegon/Bimin valley area and surrounds were there, a crowd of faces, many of them coloured in yellow ochre, a sign of mourning. We discovered that they had been on a fast since the accident and would not break their fasting until they could do so with the pilot's families now, a week later. I began to feel the level of identification these people felt towards their MAF friends and frankly, I was blown away by it.

At one stage I saw some men with jet black colouring smeared on their faces. I asked, "Why the black and not yellow ochre?"

---

1. The STOL (Short Take Off and Landing) kit added wing features such as drooping leading edge and ailerons that also acted as flaps to allow the aircraft to take off and land at a reduced speed, thus allowing it to operate to shorter runways.

"We are the men who carried the bodies of the pilots across from the crash site," one of them told me. "We crossed a creek and washed the pilot's blood covered bodies in the water. Then we scooped up the black silt in the riverbed and smeared it on our faces."

I was lost for words. Such amazing identification in grief.

After a ceremony when members of the community and family were able to share some thoughts, local food was shared, the fast broken, and we boarded the aircraft and flew across to Tekin, just a few minutes and two narrow valleys higher up the mountain range.

Tekin is one of the more challenging airstrips in the mountains of PNG. Carved into the steep side of an east-west mountain range, its notoriety with pilots comes from the unpredictable winds which flow either up or down the mountain side, creating up and down drafts at will. In earlier years a curfew by 9am was common due to the increasing tail winds often experienced on take-off. These days only more experienced pilots fly there. A short one-way airstrip (530m) with a slope of 9%, it ended in a rock wall.

While based at Telefomin and then Wewak with MAF between 1981-83, I had flown into Tekin many times, often flying produce out to the coastal base where highland vegetables were prized. At 5,500' elevation above sea level, our Wewak based, normally aspirated Cessnas were already short of breath when taking off from Tekin with a load of produce.

There were three windsocks, at the top, middle and end of the airstrip. Many a time all three pointed in different directions! It was normal to be lined up ready to take off, waiting until the windsocks turned in our favour before applying full power. Too frequently a quick look at the windsock again when about to lift off confirmed that the wind had changed again, and we would ride with the aircraft down into the valley with the tailwind, until fortune and the wind allowed us to start ascending again. It demanded the utmost from our skills.

One senior pilot recalled the time the downdraught on final approach took him down into the valley below the level of the airstrip before an updraught thankfully lifted him up again. My own moment of terror came when an updraught carried me higher on final approach. I knew that by that stage of the approach I risked hitting trees on the steep mountainside if I tried to abort the landing and go round, especially if, or when, the updraught became a downdraught. I successfully persevered with the landing, but only after using full flap and sideslip to get back on to an acceptable final approach profile. I was very thankful that I had learnt and become proficient in using sideslip, not routinely taught in flying training in modern aircraft, when flying my father's Jodel D11, which had no flaps.

A second more interesting moment of terror came on another flight when a very large pig walked onto the airstrip at my touchdown point just as I was on short final. Once again, I had no opportunity to go round. I had to land but the question was, where?

I sometimes ask people now, "What direction will a pig run if frightened – ahead or back from where it came?" I had no idea of the answer as I plotted my landing while only seconds away from touchdown. If I land over the top of the pig, the airstrip is too short and I will hit the rock wall at the end. If I land behind it, will it run into me and cause significant damage to the aircraft and possibly the occupants? I decided on the spur of the moment to land to the left of it, touching down as late as possible beside it, with my wing tip brushing the long grass in the bush beside the runway strip.

The pig stayed where she was and the landing was successful.

It did cause a more thorough approach to the perennial problem in PNG of pigs on the airstrip. The pig was killed and I presume a feast was held to honour and eat her that night! Certainly a regime declaring that any pig seen on the airstrip would be killed was now squarely in place.

Our Min friends who are watching us land and take off all the time, as well as flying in the aircraft with us, know and respect the skill level of their pilots. But it's the relationships that the pilots form with people at the airstrip communities that is much more significant. And it was that relationship that people came to honour. The wind was good and as we flew down final approach at Tekin, I could see a mass of brown faces, hundreds of people waiting beside the airstrip at the touchdown end. As we pulled into the parking area near the top of the airstrip, the mass of people as one came surging up the airstrip towards us. In different circumstances it could have been frightening.

As they reached us, the people began to spread out, forming a semi-circle around us. Chairs were brought out and we sat with our backs to the aircraft with the hoard in front. Several small coffin replicas were brought out and placed on the ground in front of us. One by one, members of the community came forward to place money in the coffins, with a short speech and gifts from the community to support the pilots' families at this time. It was an another incredible and moving expression of identification and generosity, born out of their own grief. Several thousand kina was donated.

Then I was singled out and presented with a traditional *bilum* (string bag) which was placed around my neck. It was made of 'bush rope', bark which had been rubbed and twinned, and coloured by natural ochres. Strings had been allowed to hang down about 10 cm from the base of the bag, which was quite unique. Inside the bilum some money had been placed as a donation specifically to MAF, 1,500 kina (roughly AU$800). Once again, we were being blown away by this expression of caring.

As westerners we often adopt a mindset which too often sees others as in need of our help. Whether it is colonialism or paternalism or both, it is a mindset that traps us into seeing others, particularly in cultural contexts different to ours, as needing our welfare. Unfortunately, it is also a pattern that those who become the recipients can adopt, very happy to receive what we want to give them, even an expectation of receiving. So it is such a revelation when we find ourselves being the receiver of generosity from those we thought needed ours. For this remote Tekin community, extremely poor in financial terms, to be giving so generously was an eye opener in re-evaluating our own attitudes. It was, in short, a huge blessing because it was a demonstration of the value of the relationships and their desire to contribute into those relationships. The *bilum* became my constant companion and remains a prized possession of mine to this day.

The pilots' families and relatives experienced similar expressions of grief and support at several other airstrip communities. I'm sure this must have been such an encouragement to them at this time of loss, knowing the respect and esteem with which Chris and Richard were held by the PNG communities, and the witness to Christ that accompanied it.

"MAF has lost five pilots on Min soil now, will you be pulling out of the Min area?" one community leader back at Telefomin asked me, suggesting that the cost to continue flying there had become too high. It was the question that had been on everyone's face as we travelled around the area.

"We are down two pilots and one aircraft so our ability to serve you has been reduced, but our commitment has not," I responded. "We will do what we can to continue, but it will be a reduced service from Mt Hagen and Wewak until we have more resource capacity again."

He looked relieved, but the reality of the situation was bleak for our Min friends. Telefomin and the other airstrip communities are all situated in steep-sided mountain valleys which have no road access in or out to the rest of the world. The Telefomin valley is leached, sandy soil which is constantly washed by the regular downpours of rain which these westernmost mountains of PNG are known for. Tabubil, for example, just over the ranges from Telefomin, has an annual rainfall of around 40 feet! Village people walk for hours to reach suitable garden habitat usually on the mountain sides of the valley. So supplies of basics such as rice, flour, sugar, oil and so on for the local trade stores are essential items. Everything has to be flown in, and MAF has played the major role in that for decades.

Market seller, Telefomin.
(From original watercolour)

The community meets the pilots' families at Wobegon airstrip.

Yellow ochre on the faces of the Wobegon community.

7. PILOT DEBRIEFING

Shortly after the accident, once enough information had been gleaned from the accident site to gain a preliminary understanding of what had happened, a meeting of the pilots was held in Mt Hagen. A full investigation would be made, including by the civil aviation authorities, and a report released in time. The meeting was organised by the senior pilots, headed by the Chief Pilot. It was, I thought, to provide support for the pilots in the immediate aftermath of the accident.

Management of MAF in PNG was focused on a Leadership Team, headed by the General Manager, with Chief Pilot, Chief Engineer, Finance Manager and Administration Manager, and others co-opted as needed. Apart from being thrust together as part of the accident Emergency Response Team, I had not even had opportunity to sit down and start working with some of these department heads. But I did not see the General Manager's role as micro-managing department heads or the affairs of their department. Rather they were responsible to conduct the business of their department, while Leadership Team meetings provided opportunity to review and discuss policy directions and practical solutions to issues as they raised them. From the start I felt humbled to be asked to lead this multi-cultural team of men, as all the pilots were men at that point in time, thoroughly competent and professional in their areas of expertise. They were also brothers in Christ with a depth of spiritual commitment. Over the period of the next three years, Australia, New Zealand, UK, Germany, USA, Canada and PNG would be represented in the nationalities of Leadership Team members.

I remember the pilots' meeting for two reasons particularly. I attended it because not only was I an 8,000+ hour pilot with 10 years of flying experience in MAF, but as General Manager I wished to identify with the pilots in their grief and benefit from the briefing being given them. As we sat round in a sort of circle round the room ready to start the meeting, one senior person suddenly posed a question to the group. Did they want me to be there given this was a meeting of pilots?

The question stung me and I was taken aback. The implication that I should not be there because I was now management had suddenly created a tension, a disunity, a 'them and us' moment. I was horrified at the suggestion and horrified that so quickly I was being perceived as 'them'. It cut to the heart of who I was and what I was trying to do. There was some discussion of which I remember little but I made it very clear that I was entitled as a pilot at least to be at the meeting, and I would be remaining, which I did. I was not going to become a victim of this divisive mentality so early in my appointment, nor the idea that 'management' should not be entitled to know what was going on.

All the pilots were devastated by the loss of their mates. The senior pilots, leading the meeting, were particularly upset - understandably, for this accident had happened on their watch. Most accidents occur because there has been a breakdown of procedures at some point in time during events leading up to or during a flight. Sometimes it can happen long before the pilots actually get into the aircraft, and a mechanical defect or failure places them in a compromised safety situation. In this case, Chris and Richard were flying lower than usual presumably to try and see under the ground fog which was over the airstrip itself. As a result, it appeared that some circuit area standard operating procedures (SOPs) needed reinforcing.[2] In their grief and frustration over the result, the meeting became an opportunity to reinforce the need to maintain SOPs, rather than an opportunity to share their grief together.

Later feedback from some pilots confirmed what I was feeling and that the meeting had not been as helpful as it could have been for them. I don't say this to be critical of the senior pilots, who were also trying to find their feet as responsible leaders in the midst of their grief. Rather it provided for me a valuable management lesson.

Sometimes those who are most involved in, closest to, or responsible in a situation, particularly when it is stressful or involves conflict or trauma, are best to step aside from their involvement while the situation is being resolved. I made up my own mind that if there was ever a next time, I would ensure that the responsibility for this early counselling for pilots and technical staff was handled by someone else, a third party who understood the situation well but was not so personally involved.

---

2. Following this accident, SOPs were introduced stipulating minimum criteria for landing including stabilised approach by 300'.

Typical Pilot's meeting, MAF PNG, Mt Hagen. These brothers in Christ represented the most skilled pilots found anywhere in the world to carry out God's mission through MAF in PNG.

GA8 Airvan at Lapalama, Enga Province, looking down the one way airstrip.

8. HIJACK THREATS

Someone was rattling the front gate near our house on our MAF residential compound. I ventured out to see who it was. Giri had turned up again, wanting to speak with me. He held a hand-written letter which he wanted me to read. It alleged that there was a plot by *raskal* gangsters to hijack an MAF aircraft from a Western Province lowland's base and land it at a disused airstrip in the Southern Highlands. The offenders would be carrying guns, smuggled in presumably from Indonesia, which borders on the Western Province.

I was hesitant to put any credibility on this letter and suspected that Giri had developed this elaborate scheme to ultimately improve his own well-being. We were already familiar with the kinds of untruths that people peddled in their efforts to secure some benefit for themselves. Some years earlier, while living in Port Moresby, I had been amazed when a man came begging for money at my house one day, somewhat arrogantly saying he was needing financial assistance for bus fares to his wife's village. As the story went, he had cut her hand off following a dispute and spent some time in prison as a result, was now released and heading off to her village. I strongly suspected that his wife's family may not be agreeable to his visit and so the story failed to impress me. I offered him some food, which he promptly threw into the front garden bed as he walked off the property!

I needed to test if there was any validity to the threat that Giri had raised. How had he come to receive this information? I queried.

It was through his own network of contacts in the *raskal* gangs. Right, so it was clear that he was a bona fide *raskal* himself. He must have figured that the benefit from such a betrayal of his *raskal* mates like this would ultimately be better for himself, probably a risky assumption!

I asked him if he would be happy to personally verify the letter, to which he replied, "Yes".

I asked him if he would be prepared to go as far as showing it to the Police, to which he again said, "Yes".

Would he be willing to speak with the Commissioner for Police to authenticate the letter and its threat? Again he replied, "Yes".

This now presented me with a dilemma, as the Police Commissioner was in Port Moresby. The only way to travel there was by aircraft (airline generally) and that would cost a considerable amount of money for return flights for us both. Moreover, it would confirm my belief that this story was true – something I was still quite unsure about. At what point would Giri change his story or disappear?

I contacted the Police Commissioner's office and discovered that he was actually visiting Goroka over the next couple of days. This presented a much more practical option. Goroka was about 30 minutes flying down the Waghi Valley from Mt Hagen. While something like a half day trip one way by car or PMV (public motor vehicle bus), a return trip in just a couple of hours could be easily achieved by light aircraft, with minimum expense.

So it was that a few days later, having arranged for a quick meeting in the field at Goroka with the Police Commissioner, I strapped Giri into a Cessna at Mt Hagen's Kagamuga airport and flew him to Goroka to meet the Commissioner. By the time we landed half an hour later, I was feeling much more confident that Giri's claim about the proposed hijacking was true. He had too much at stake now for it to be falsehood.

We met briefly with the Commissioner, told him the story and showed him the letter, and left the matter in his hands, flying back to Mt Hagen soon after.

While the Police may be investigating, we now had a critical situation to address. The risks were real and high. People boarding an aircraft with guns concealed in bags or clothing were a real risk. We had already been moving to introduce hand-held scanners for airport security staff to check all passengers before boarding.

Over the course of the next three years there would be a number of times when security alerts were issued to be on the lookout for passengers concealing weapons. Some concealments were an outrage, such as women hiding weapons under their oversize 'meri blouse', or a dismantled semi-automatic hidden underneath a sleeping baby in its *bilum*.

For an aircraft to be hijacked in flight would be traumatic and possibly life-threatening for the pilot and any passengers on board. There have been a couple of hijacks that MAF pilots have experienced over the years and fortunately none resulted in loss of life though the pilots were traumatised. Add to this the threat of landing at a disused jungle airstrip that was not up to an acceptable standard. That could subject the aircraft to significant damage, and those on board to serious risk of injury or worse.

So the question of how we deal with this possible hijack situation became a major issue on the agenda of our Leadership Team meeting. MAF had one aircraft based in the Western Province, providing services to nearly 200,000 people in their village communities over an area of nearly 1,000,000 hectares. With few roads, lots of jungle and swampland, the aircraft was a lifeline for these communities, churches and missionaries. For their sake, we could not afford to close down our operation, yet on the other hand, we could not continue to operate unless we knew the risk of a hijack was removed. The risk for the pilot, passengers and aircraft was too high to play games.

So it was with much regret that I informed the pilot that we were to cease flying out of Western Province ports until the matter was resolved. He found being grounded frustrating, knowing that the whole community was being held ransom already by having no flights. More stringent security screening arrangements were put into place and once we were fully able to be confident that the risk of hijack was now minimal, we recommenced flying again, about two weeks later. No hijack eventuated.

Sometime later, when I enquired of the Police as to the follow-up from Giri's statement, I was told that Police operations had uncovered some gun smuggling gangs out of Kiunga, but no details were able to be shared. There was acknowledgement that Giri's information had been valuable to Police in their efforts.

Over the course of time Giri continued to visit me occasionally, even attended church a few times at my encouragement. I thanked him for his assistance and his duty of care towards his countrymen but did not offer him any reward for his information, though did seek to help him out personally with some clothes. However, I had to draw a line on this when his persistence began to overwhelm me. Sometime later, again at the front gate, I had to advise him that, as he was already wearing my shirt on his back and my shoes on his feet, there was nothing more that I could help him with. He needed to find his own way forward now.

I felt disappointed that I could not help him more but when relationships become unhealthy, with people just hanging on to draw what they can out of you, they have to be released.

Trekking out through leech infested jungle to inspect a new airstrip some years earlier, I witnessed first hand the way my PNG colleagues dealt with the leeches crawling up their legs (mine were in my socks!). Using their razor-sharp machetes, the leeches were swiftly dispatched with a deft slide of the blade flat down the side of their leg.

Unfortunately the cut off point had come for Giri. The line between tough love and cold-heartedness seems thin sometimes.

The Price of a Plane

The price of a plane can often seem high,
When we look at the alternatives to travel by;
It costs nothing to walk but the sweat on our brow,
And the hours and days ahead of us now.
But what about where there is no track?
Tall mountains and valleys and jungle set us back;
For the nearest mountain range is one day away -
In a plane it's only three minutes, they say!

The price of a plane can often seem high,
But its safety and speed one cannot deny.
In a land such as this where rivers abound,
The canoe is not a bad way to get around;
It's cheap, though slow, pretty hot in the sun,
And quite tiring when the day is done.
But there's crocodiles, and rapids, and flash floods aren't new
And it seems the dangers are more than a few!

The price of a plane can often seem high,
When it's with dollars and cents we buy;
But can money really measure the cost...
Of reaching a tribe still lost?
For the man whose life has been snatched by a snake,
A couple of hours is all he will take;
Or the trauma of childbirth and its toll on a wife -
Why, the price of a plane is the price of life!

Copyright © 1981 Michael Jelliffe

9. AIRCRAFT IN, AIRCRAFT OUT

Many things were changing in MAF. At an international level, MAF Aus/NZ was moving to merger with other MAFs around the world to form a global MAF International. There were signs of that happening, one of the most visible was the introduction of a new colour scheme. Instead of the yellow, brown and white which had been MAF Aus/NZ trademark colours for aircraft, uniforms and stationary, shades of blue, red and white were replacing the old. Nowhere was this more obvious than in the introduction of staff uniforms of light and navy blue, and in the new colour scheme for aircraft - white with a line of red and blue expanding down the fuselage. It certainly did look brighter. MAF International formally commenced in September 2006.

There was also a move to introduce new aircraft types into the operation. For several years MAF Australia/NZ had been working closely with Gippsland Aeronautics in Victoria developing a new aircraft type suitable for bush operations, a kind of Aussie airborne 'ute'. MAF had been able to have some input into technical and practical aspects of the aircraft, to be called the GA8 Airvan.

While the trustworthy Cessna 206 had been a stable workhorse for decades, the GA8 provided the promise of similar STOL[3] performance and an enlarged cabin with six

---
3. STOL - Short Take Off and Landing

individual seats plus co-pilot's seat, and a large sliding door. The seats could be easily removed and stored in the rear section behind the cabin, and the cabin configured for freight consignments including on pallets.

The first GA8 Airvan to enter MAF PNG service arrived during the third quarter of 2005, registered P2-MFE, resplendent in the new blue, red and white colour scheme. There was great anticipation of its arrival and of the value it would add to the operation. People had gathered at the hangar in Mt Hagen once the arrival time was known early in the afternoon. Having flown from Mareeba, near Cairns, up to Thursday Island to clear customs, and then to Mt Hagen via Daru, it was welcomed by an arch of water spray from the airport Fire Service tender as it taxied in. Soon after we held a formal commissioning of the aircraft to service.

MAF has depended by and large on donations to purchase new aircraft and this was no exception. The Evangelical Lutheran Church (ELC) in Bavaria had donated the funds to purchase the aircraft from the factory, and representatives were on hand for the commissioning. A decal advising of their stake in the aircraft proudly announced this to everyone boarding the aircraft, stuck on the side of the aircraft. MAF PNG had supported the ministry of ELC for many years but the real need was in the Lae and surrounding Morobe districts. So this aircraft carried with it some expectation of MAF being able to increase its service capacity to those areas.

There was constant shuffling and reshuffling required to maintain consistency of service as needs around the country varied and pilots came and went on holidays or longer periods of furlough. We also sought to give pilots exposure to expanding areas of PNG at different bases as their experience broadened. These issues were often at the forefront of Leadership Team meeting agenda.

MAF was also reviewing its vision and purpose, with a view to understanding how it could be more strategic in its role. While a very practical ministry of transportation at a purely pragmatic level, our main focus was still to assist the churches and missions in their ministries in isolated and remote areas. So our priority needed to be not on how many hours flying we did, though we would still measure that, but on how effective our ministry is in bringing about spiritual transformation in those people and communities we engaged with.

So I approached the experienced pilot family at Kawito, Michael and Jenny, with a new challenge to commence the Lae operation with the new GA8 Airvan. They loved Kawito and had made amazing relationships there, but reluctantly agreed to relocate to the Lae area, where they quickly established relationships and a valid flight program. Another newer family, Chris and Narelle and their young children, replaced them at Kawito.

Unfortunately the toll in maintenance on aircraft operating into rough bush airstrips, most with a grassed surface but sometimes gravelled, is high. Occasionally the damage to an aircraft would be more severe and require expensive and extensive maintenance or repair. When one C206 aircraft suffered extensive damage landing at a difficult airstrip in the Sepik, we were thankful that the pilot and passengers were not injured, though the aircraft was a write-off.

In another incident a C206 slid off the side of a slippery airstrip and ended up one wing down in undergrowth beside the strip. No one was injured but the aircraft required considerable maintenance. The challenge of getting a damaged aircraft into Mt Hagen for repairs is huge, and may require airlift by a large helicopter. We appreciated the Australian Defence

Force assisting to bring a wingless C206 into Mt Hagen from Telefomin, wheeled into a military transport aircraft!

We had also experienced more than one 'prop-strike', when a propeller had hit the ground, usually because the nose wheel has sunk into a soft patch on the runway or taxiway surface. The difficulty here was that if the propeller was under power at the time of impact, then there was potential for internal damage to the engine. So a strip down of the engine followed by rigorous testing of components was required before rebuild. With any additional maintenance or repair, the result was an aircraft out of service for an extended time, reducing our fleet availability.

Much as the new GA8 added to the fleet, the earlier loss of the Twin Otter, then a C206 as well as extended maintenance or repairs on others, kept us still at minimum fleet capacity. Another operator's misfortune became our blessing though. We purchased a C206 which had sustained some nose gear damage landing at a remote airstrip, and commenced a repair and refurbishment of it, to become P2-MFO.

Three aircraft types in operation - C206, GA8 Airvan & DHC6.

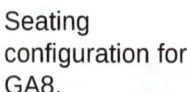

Commissioning for P2-MFE, Mt Hagen hangar.

Large sliding cargo door on GA8 allowing loading of bulky items.

Seating configuration for GA8.

10. PRACTICAL RESPONSES TO SPIRITUAL THREATS

Two longer term issues arose now following the accident. We were now two pilots and one aircraft short yet the demand for our services had not diminished. For many communities we were the only contact with the outside world. Already pilot numbers were below optimal levels for an operation the size of MAFs in PNG with over a dozen aircraft. How would we respond to the loss of the aircraft internally, and how would we respond to the Min community who now had no pilots or aircraft to operate their area?

Back in my office I had a call from some local pastors who wished to come and see me. So we set up a meeting time in my office. As we sat together, they shared that it had been revealed to them that there was a concerted satanic effort to destroy the work of MAF in PNG. The accident had provided the opportunity for this to become obvious, perhaps even the start of an evil offensive. They offered their support and fellowship in prayer, something I appreciated immensely. They saw us as partners in ministry for the benefit of the gospel in PNG, and any disruption to this ministry was going to be a direct attack on the gospel it represented. They would be partners in prayer with and for MAF.

I came out of that meeting with a much clearer understanding of the spiritual nature of our ministry, and a determined conviction that MAF would not be destroyed on my watch as field leader. That conviction would be put to the test soon after but in the meantime one of our national staff came to see me. She'd had a dream which had convinced her that satan was seeking to destroy MAF. She had no idea about the visit I had from the pastors and it just made my resolution to see God's will through MAF achieved even stronger. What an amazing fellowship we were privileged to be part of, with national pastors and staff giving us clear spiritual insight on the intentions of the enemy.

The Leadership Team met to discuss a way forward. As pilot recruitment was done in the home countries, not PNG, recruiting efforts were to be emphasized to reduce the pilot shortage. There is no quick fix, fly by night short cut to recruitment. Typically, once a pilot has trained for a Commercial Pilot Licence and gained some flying experience, then they must pass an MAF flight check. This covers not only actual flying skills but aspects such as attitudes and emotional intelligence. Then medical checks for suitability for tropical and cross-cultural living, and others which cover Christian maturity and spiritual gifts are conducted. Most applicants have spent a year or more at a Bible College. So this process can take up to five years or more.

The Twin Otter aircraft lost in the accident is a workhorse, known worldwide for its rugged ability to operate in the bush. MAF was operating four such aircraft at the time. It could carry about three times the payload of the smaller single engine Cessna 206 (and later GA Airvan) aircraft which were the mainstay of flight operations for decades, and fly in cloud (IFR), prohibited in single engine aircraft. Losing one aircraft had a huge impact on our capacity to serve the rural communities. So the question of whether we should seek to replace the aircraft with another Twin Otter, or just downsize to the three remaining Twin Otters had to be addressed.

The Leadership Team that met to discuss this had five members in attendance. Discussion continued for some time as we wrestled with this issue which would have a profound impact of our ability to continue to serve. The issue to me was clear. To not replace the aircraft would be admitting defeat in the spiritual battle we were engaged in. When it came time to vote, the meeting was split 2 for replacement, and 2 against. Feelings were strong on both sides, but the deciding vote was mine. I unashamedly chose to say that we must replace the aircraft. MAF leadership was advised of our decision and supported it accordingly.

Of course, making a decision like that and making it happen are two different things. It was a massive step of faith. The cost of these aircraft because of their popularity worldwide is high. Those that are cheaper have high airframe hours and probably need scheduled maintenance such as wing modifications, major airframe checks, or have high hour engines. Some of the Twin Otters operated by MAF have accumulated nearly 40,000 flying hours. They continue only because of continued diligent maintenance and replacement of time limited parts. For us to get a replacement Twin Otter would be nothing short of a miracle.

Something amazing began to happen. A spark of spiritual hope was ignited and, rising from the ashes of the accident, a new wave of hope began to rise. People took this challenge on and began praying. I remember so well the enthusiasm by so many of our PNG staff in Mt Hagen. We were not going to accept defeat.

Then we received news that not one, but two Twin Otter aircraft had been located for sale in USA. Both had been used sporadically for rain seeding in China (the manuals had to be translated into English!) and so they had only around 6,000 airframe hours, well below anything we could have expected. This news ignited the groundswell of prayer and excitement. Suddenly there was an enthusiasm and hope, and small groups of people could be found gathered in prayer, even in the hangar where they were meant to be at work! But this was real work and God was already providing!

We prayed for funds to be received to top up the insurance payout. Then we heard that funds to purchase one aircraft had been received by MAF head office. The senior Engineer, Larry, a highly qualified and experienced Twin Otter mechanic and pilot, went across to inspect the aircraft. Several months later, once formalities and the installation of fuel tanks which took up the whole cabin area were completed, the Chief Pilot, Lowell, flew one across the Pacific, in company with a second Cessna Caravan aircraft destined for MAF in Irian Jaya, Indonesia. Registered as P2-MFT, it became for me and many, a symbol of victory in the battle against spiritual darkness.

Resplendent in a fresh new blue and red stripped colour scheme, its commissioning on the 14th October, 2005, was a time of great release and pride. The hangar was decked out with a huge red curtain hiding the aircraft until it was pulled back to showcase. Various leaders came to the event, including most members of the MAF PNG Board, MAF Australia Board Chairman Russell Stebbins and CEO Bill Harding, as well as MAF UK Chairman, Alan Devereux, most of whom spoke at the event. Rev Dr Joshua Daimoi, senior Christian statesman and MAF PNG Board member, gave an address.

In our efforts to improve staff morale and look, Kathy and I had embarked on a project to see staff in uniforms. We had purchased material during a visit to Port Moresby and Kathy had cut and sown red, blue and white patterned scarves for the female staff, to complement their light blue blouses and dark blue skirts. It was a huge success. We just felt and shared their pride as they showcased their uniforms publicly during the commissioning. We felt that what the Lord did through the coming of this aircraft was so helpful in destroying some of the negativity and despair that had come from the accident. Some staff still have their scarves as a wonderful reminder of that time. We also took the opportunity to honour our team by presenting awards to many of them.

MAF PNG Board - (rear left) Ps Martin Wayne, Ogla Makindi, Bill Harding, David Sode, Ps David Muap, Alan Devereux (MAF UK), (Front left) Rev Dr Joshua Damoi, Mr Russell Stebbins, myself.

MAF PNG Engineering team.

Commissioning Ceremony for P2-MFT.

Female staff in uniform.

Twin Otter P2-MFT outside Mt Hagen hangar.

Ben Agerenga, Chief Engineer, receives his award from MAF Aus Chairman Russell Stebbins.

11. RESPONDING TO THE MIN COMMUNITY

To answer the second question and our response to the Min community, we were able to immediately keep flying to the area with a Twin Otter from our Mt Hagen or Goroka base, with the pilots often overnighting for one or two nights a week. It was a minimal service but all we could manage. At least it kept up some visibility and service as the aircraft flew in and out of the airstrips. In these locations, everyone hears the aircraft and knows who it belongs to.

Aware of all the assistance provided by the community in the Wobegon/Bimin valley during the recovery, we sought to do something which would be of benefit to the community. As we reached out to them for feedback, the need for a health aid post building became clear. We approved the project at Leadership Team level but it took some time before we were able to work out the logistics, such as the opportunity to buy locally milled timber, and flying in the hardware needed to build from scratch. Eventually a team of MAF volunteers flew in for a weekend in the bush at Wobegon and constructed the simple building, working alongside the local community. It was one way for us to give something back to this community and say thank you.

A few months after the accident, one of the pilots who was out at Telefomin contacted me to advise of some disturbing reports. A large gathering of local community members had met at the Telefomin community hall and begun to air their grievances over the lack of service MAF was now able to provide. Voices had been raised; threats possibly made.

During the drier season, staple crops like sweet potato are difficult to grow and people have to walk further away from the village and town area, often spending one or two nights at their gardens higher up on the mountains. The town was also home to a number of people from other areas of PNG, now working in government, business, health or education roles. They were very dependent on buying local produce. Now in the midst of such a dry season, the tradestore shelves were almost empty, and people were struggling. MAF had not been able to maintain enough transportation to keep store stocks up to meet demand. The locals were rightly fighting to get basic supply chains functioning as a matter of urgency.

From my previous experience in Telefomin, both as the pilot based there and the recent visits following the accident, I felt a level of understanding of their concerns. I also knew that in PNG discussion and negotiation comes before the bows and arrows are drawn; relationships are everything. I advised the pilot to let the community leaders know that I would visit for a community meeting as soon as it could be arranged. The following week I boarded our flight from Mt Hagen for Telefomin.

People from all walks of life and work had gathered in the community hall in preparation. Was I walking into a situation of great danger? I could only go on my instincts that said, this might be a spiritual issue at heart but it needed diplomacy at a relational level to resolve.

As our flight taxied into the parking bay, I could see people up at the community hall. I grabbed my bag and just as I started to walk up the hill to the hall, an older man was walking past. He stopped and looked at me.

"Oh, it's you is it," he said to me with a slight grin. "I remember having a meal with you when you were based here. I'll walk up with you."

That simple nostalgic encounter took away my fears. I was among friends and as I prepared to enter the lion's den, that's how I would approach the meeting.

The hall was crowded, with people milling around outside as well. I made my way inside, aware that there was only one white face in the hall - mine. The key to resolving conflict and negotiation is to listen lots, speak little; come with an open mind and heart, not a closed fist; be ready to compromise so that both sides can win. I also know that in Melanesia, consensus is achieved through listening to all parties. I've seen first speakers in a discussion reiterate their strong viewpoint on an issue, only to change their opinion 180 degrees once they had heard the others speak. One of the things I had come to admire in Melanesians is the humility that says, it's ok to change your opinion when you hear the wisdom of the group. So I would start by listening.

After introductions, and before saying too much myself, I asked to hear what different people from the community wished to say. I sensed there was no antagonism, no threat here, I was with friends, and I wanted to hear their voice.

Various people from the community spoke, mostly in Tok Pisin, expressing the hardships the community was experiencing. I began to recognise different corners of the community being highlighted – health care (there is a mission - church run health and nurse training facility), education (Telefomin has a high school), local businesses, local government, and community at large. I guess we spent over an hour together allowing one after another of those present to speak on behalf of their corner. While there might have been anger at their earlier meeting, it was just sharing from the heart this time, and that allowed people to be overly expressive if they needed to be! There's nothing wrong with sharing your hardship with passion!

Once I was confident that all who wished to speak had been able to share, I found myself wondering how to respond. It was a pensive and scary moment, with a hall full of frustrated people wanting answers. I can only believe that God provided inspiration at the critical point. I knew I needed to give the people something positive that they could leave this hall with. I couldn't promise more airplanes and pilots. I couldn't promise any quick fix solutions except perhaps a few extra flights to try and top up the tradestores, which I did. But I could do something else with more long-lasting results.

I made a bold suggestion, and it sought to meet the real need behind the expressed need, and that was to be able to communicate what they were going through with us.

"I'd like to make a suggestion," I said to the group, in Tok Pisin, "Why don't you appoint a person from each corner of the community, representing the various sectors we have heard from today, and form a committee to represent you all. I'll come and meet with you here in Telefomin regularly to listen to you and make sure MAF can target your needs in the community."

Thus the Min Balus Committee (*balus* is aircraft in Tok Pisin) was birthed and a new relationship with the Min community was formed. This had to be a slap in the face of those who may have sought our decline or destruction.

I aimed to attend Min Balus Committee meetings every three to six months and was able to continue that over the next two years until others took my place. Represented on it were local political and administrative heads as well as people with links to health, church, education and business. A sign stating Min Balus Project was displayed in the District Office administration building where we would meet.

Discussion at the meetings over time began to turn to matters expressing the community's aspirations to have control over their own air operation, with the focus on purchasing an aircraft. My response was to encourage their vision but remind them that they also needed pilots to fly the aircraft. My recommendation was that they use their resources initially to sponsor one or two of their younger generation for pilot training with the MAF flying school in Mt Hagen. Then they would be in a better position to purchase and operate an aircraft successfully. After a lifetime of seeing aircraft coming and going from their airstrips, most rural communities in PNG have a desire to operate their own aircraft.

It was decided that a small contribution of ten kina (~$4) be sought from people throughout the Min area to finance the Min Balus Committee aspirations, and a fund was established. Over time, politicians also arranged funding into the Committee coffers. The funds and political connections grew though no pilot training was initiated by the time I concluded my tenure as MAF PNG General Manager and member of the MBC.

One significant event which demonstrated again to me the value and depth of the relationships MAF people have established in the community came when the former Prime Minister, Grand Chief Sir Michael Somare, visited Telefomin on the 16th February, 2007. A week or two before that I had received an invitation from the Committee to come to Telefomin for this event. The Grand Chief, who was one of the key political players when the country received Independence in 1975 and in the years since, was loved and highly respected throughout PNG. His arrival brought great jubilation, with local groups in their local *bilas* (decorations) performing dances as he disembarked our Twin Otter aircraft which had flown him in.

As we moved into the community hall, crowded inside and outside, I was ushered inside and then to my surprise, told to go onstage and sit next to the Prime Minister. It was an unexpected moment of extreme privilege for me. No other expatriates were visible in the hall. I was asked to give a speech and used it (again in Tok Pisin) to encourage the Prime Minister to consider the real needs of the local community, praising them as a community of good, resourceful people with aspirations, but going through tough times. During his speech, Sir Michael looked over to me at one point and made reference to former MAF pilots who were well known to him. I knew that he was referring to Max Meyers and others of the early MAF pioneers who would have known him as a young politician in the East Sepik. It has been moments like these in my time in PNG that have been etched into my memory as historical markers, giving me immense pride and joy by being accepted so openly into these amazing PNG communities.

The Min Balus Committee in the years following my departure did go on to purchase an aircraft (a PAC 750) and operate it in the Min area under an arrangement with an existing commercial operator. Yes, they had political intrusion and money problems, and an accident at one stage, so it has been a rocky road at times. But I am happy to think that out of our accident was birthed something that was able to empower the community by giving them a vehicle to realise their own aspirations and find solutions to their own problems. That to me is at the heart of what community development really is.

Min Balus Project collection point and some of the committee at the District Administration building, Telefomin, including District Administrator and Local Level Govt President.
(Note my prized Tekin bilum on my shoulder).

After the community meeting at Telefomin (myself right rear).

Meeting Grand Chief Sir Michael Somare, who had just arrived in Telefomin from Vanimo on P2-MFT.

12. RECRUITMENT, HIV & BIRD FLU

When I first took over as General Manager, I was aware of some local staffing situations that needed to be addressed. In one instance, I knew I had to make a decision about a local female staff member who was creating discontent among her team and acting in a bullying manner at times. I recognised that she would probably seek to legally challenge any action which she did not like, especially if she felt it was not fully legal. She was not on a contract and as we were moving to having staff on contacts, I negotiated a one-year employment contract with her. At the end of that year her contract was not renewed as there had been no change in attitudes.

Sometime later I received a visit from government Labour department officials who had received a complaint that a local person had been fired so that an expatriate could take her place. There are strict rules in PNG regarding employment, including jobs that cannot be held by expatriates, who must have a work permit for a specific role. This basis of this complaint was untrue, however the officials thought they smelled a rat and wanted to do a thorough search through all our employment records, including expatriate work permits. I openly welcomed their scrutiny but drew the line when they wanted to take our files with them. I said they were very welcome to review them on-site though. There was some uneasiness evident during the visit and I wondered where they would take the issue.

Sometime later I had further contact with them. They started the conversation by acknowledging the fact that things hadn't started off on a good footing at the previous meeting, however they wished to correct that and there had been no ongoing issues for them in the matter. Contact with them after this was both helpful and cordial. The irony is that a year or two later, MAF PNG received formal recognition by the government for its employment relations in the form of a Good Corporate Citizenship award, which included granting improved status when applying for work permits.

I felt vindicated when I later found out that the staff member concerned had been communicating unwisely with one of our single missionary pilots.

As the year progressed, I continued to look for the additional management staff we needed. The signs from Australia were not good. Recruitment so far had yielded no management workers, especially no Executive Officer who could work with me.

Recognising that I would need to recruit within PNG, I made some changes and introduced new staff. The Administration Manager, Kos Umion (from West Sepik), a former Air Traffic Controller, moved to take up the Ground Operations position. I hired a new Administration Manager, Eric Eribiang (Western Highlands), a former Post Office manager with a good record. Because he was from the local area, he also became invaluable in negotiating disputes with the local community. A new Secretary for myself, Sophie, (Eastern Highlands/Milne Bay) was hired and she became a valuable member of our team over many years, later moving into more senior roles in quality management. There was also new recruitment for some of the outstation bases that MAF operated from around the country. We developed a dedicated team of good people in these roles, including Fred Orawi (Hela Province), who became a key person in Ground Operations management. All of these people became good friends and colleagues, brothers and sisters in Christ.

One of my main goals when I took on the role was to establish an effective performance management system for staff. It was evident that there was little being done to provide local staff with a functional opportunity to review their work performance, ensure it was in line with the organisation's vision and goals, and that their own interests were being met. One marker of this came, for example, when I reviewed the excessive amount of overtime being paid, especially at outstation bases. So workers were at work when there were requirements early in the morning through until last light often. The role of the base manager was critical to ensure that they rostered workers to avoid everyone being on duty all the time. The need for supervisory mentoring for middle managers was clear.

Working with Titus and Kos, we sought to introduce a monthly supervisory meeting for base managers initially. When people see management as waving a big stick at them, it creates an atmosphere of mistrust, where workers feel they are constantly being monitored for doing the wrong thing. I wanted to use a different approach, one that focused on performance management as an empowering mechanism.

The supervisory meeting would zero in on the worker's job description in the first instance and use that as a template for review. Invariably the question would come - is this what you are actually doing? Not to berate the worker but to understand better how their job description fitted into the big picture, and whether they were actually doing someone elses job description. Then, opportunity to talk over how each component was being handled would naturally lead to understanding some shortfalls in performance, if any.

But this was approached in a spirit of understanding first where the organisation was failing to equip or empower the worker to do their job - with equipment, training, rostering etc. - before considering more personal issues for which the worker was responsible. While achieving a limited measure of success with this, I was disappointed that other priorities often overtook us.[4]

PNG was in the grip of an AIDS/HIV epidemic and so we believed it would be appropriate to recruit a person to provide education for staff and in the wider community. After thinking about it for a while, one day in late May 2005 I called Kambowa, whom I had known since I started working in commercial aviation in Mt Hagen 33 years earlier. We were both young men attending the same church in Mt Hagen. He had now retired as a government Health Education Officer and was ready for a new challenge. I offered him a role as an HIV/AIDS Project Officer. It turned out that he was waiting for my call, and the day I rang him was the deadline day he had given the Lord to have us take him on!

Over a number of years Kambowa subsequently developed AIDS/HIV awareness programs for staff, even gaining a community award for workplace excellence in HIV/AIDS education. He also developed awareness and education opportunities for outreach into the local community and to remote airstrip communities, coupled with evangelistic ministry with teams of MAF staff volunteers. This was an essential element of our responsibility to the wider community. HIV/AIDS was taking a huge toll, evidenced by the increasing number of graves seen around villages by pilots from the air.

In early 2007 we received reports of Asian Bird Flu being found in remote communities near the Indonesian

---
4. I later developed this into a 5 day training course attended by all managers in MAF PNG, out of which came my book, "Leading to Empower - Biblical Perspectives on the Art of Leading and Managing People" (www.nengebooks.com).

border. The serious risk of transmission further around PNG and into Australia now prompted preventative action, with liaison between quarantine agencies in PNG and Australia. Kambowa was able to take a lead in this as well. We were contracted to conduct flights with quarantine officers to all the airstrips up and down the border. We also had to implement internal quarantine measures which included not allowing livestock transportation between provinces and maintaining appropriate cleansing of aircraft moving in and out of critical areas. It added a further level of complexity to operations.

MAF in PNG has always had a strong focus on training. In the Engineering department, a number of PNG apprentices had graduated as Licensed Aircraft Maintenance Engineers (LAME). Others were actively engaged in pursuing their apprenticeship as Aircraft Maintenance Engineers (AME). For some time after I commenced my role as GM, Ben (Eastern Highlands Province), held the position of Chief Engineer.

While operational flying as a GM was no longer permitted by MAF, I was able to fly still in a private capacity for mission business, using a C206, hired C182 or later, the flight school C172. While visiting Australia conducting a C206 ferry flight on one occasion, I made a spontaneous invitation to an administration worker (Glen) in MAF's Mareeba hangar/workshop facility - only to have her accept the offer as a Human Resources manager for international staff in PNG, a role she excelled in for many years. It might have been regarded as sheep stealing but was the beginning of a very happy sojourn for her back in PNG, where she had lived earlier - and marriage to another international staffer (Godfrey)! Titus (Milne Bay) and team were already providing HR for local staff. With over 100 Papua New Guinean staff, and around 50 international missionaries, MAF PNG was truly an international organisation.

As I got to know the PNG staff, I was always impressed by their love and commitment to Christ and to the broader community they served. I sought to get some time personally with as many as I could to build trust and confidence in my leadership. Certainly I believed that the events following the accident had done that.

From time to time I was touched by how simple acts of relationship building can be so rewarded. I had painted a watercolour picture of Paul (Southern Highlands), one of our traffic officers, with his sunglasses *(aiglas)* on, in front of a Twin Otter in our old yellow and brown colour scheme. So I made a copy, framed it and gave it to him. He is a big guy with a big heart. With tears in his eyes he said to me, "No one has even done anything like this for me before". I was touched.

Over the next few years I would work a lot with Paul in a number of projects and I knew that I always had his 100% support, and he mine. He was one of many who I would regard as good friends. For many years Paul subsequently managed MAFs fuel logistics around the bases.

On most days I tried to spend a few minutes visiting the staff at the Mt Hagen flight terminal, a seperate building several sites down from the hangar and administration offices. Martha, a faithful long term traffic officer and general assistant, had just finished telling a new staffer that I would visit soon, when I appeared from the tarmac, validating her claim. It also alerted me to the value of this relatonship building exercise.

While most training was focused on aviation related skills, we also sought to encourage those who sought training in Christian ministry, through sponsorship. Some, like Martin, had done accredited courses through Christian Leaders Training College, the country's main interdenominational Bible College at Banz about an hour's drive from Kagamuga.

Albert was an uneducated cleaner from Tari who had spent years in MAF PNG faithfully going about his cleaning duties day in, day out. But he was also pastoring a small local church and was able to commence training through one of the evangelical denominations locally in Mt Hagen to enhance his pastoral skills and Biblical understanding. It was a source of pride for all of us when he graduated. I was very pleased to be able to attend his graduation, in fact, I was invited to be the guest speaker as well.

We sought to encourage local staff welfare including through local sports competitions. This included sponsoring a women's netball team in the local Kagamuga competition, complete with uniforms. They did well in the comp too!

By early 2007 a major three yearly review of all expatriate work positions and permits for the PNG government was becoming due. One of the pilots, Derek, had expressed an interest in a management role and so I pulled him off flying and into an EO role, though his main focus was to see completion of the work permit review. This took months and he did well. Our submission was successful, but by then he was ready to get back to flying again, and so he was released back to flying (which he did for many more years).

Despite the growing levels of staff at management levels, I still found myself largely dealing with day-to-day issues. I knew that my appointment was with the intention of being able to focus on broader issues that would develop and grow the ministry of MAF PNG into the future. But the reality was still that day-to-day dramas too often took first priority. During my three years as GM, no Executive Officer was able to be recruited.

Paul 'aiglas'.
(from original watercolour)

Albert's graduation.

Paul checks the load in a GA8 Airvan for security.

Kathy with MAF PNG women's netball team.

Lucy, Executive Secretary (lt), and Sophie, Secretary to GM (rt), always ready to help.

With some of our Bases Managers and staff, running bases all over PNG.
(Fred, 2nd from left front)

Kambowa with Bird Flu and HIV/AIDS awareness material.

13. ENGAGING IN THE WIDER COMMUNITY

The wife of a local leader in the Kagamuga (Mt Hagen) airport precinct community passed away. It was a time of mourning in the community of which MAF has been a part since the 1960s, not only with accommodation compounds for missionaries but residential housing for a number of national staff.

Relationships with the local community are important and times like this provide opportunity for us to strengthen that relationship. Traditionally people make donations to the family to show their support. The MAF staff passed the hat around and raised 1,000 kina, so I doubled that as an equal MAF contribution. A ceremony was being held nearby under the yar trees to enable people to make their donations and join with the family. So I attended and was given opportunity to say a few words. Standing in the middle of a large circle of local community members, I made the donation on behalf of MAF staff and organisation. It was well received and some staff commented to me afterwards that MAF "had never done this before". If that was the case, I hoped it was the first of many more community engagements to come. We often say that relationships are everything in PNG. If that is true then we must take every opportunity to build them.

As part of my role, I liked to be able to visit our bases around the country and see how things were going and encourage the base staff with any issues they were facing. Having already flown in and out of these locations during our earlier terms of service in MAF, I felt somewhat aware of their particular contexts.

One former airstrip in the Sepik Province, Anguganak, had been closed as a MAF base for some time. Services were handled from Wewak by the Wewak pilots. However an issue arose concerning the airstrip. The community called for a meeting and I flew down, about an hour and a half flight north west from Mt Hagen. Kathy accompanied me as we were then heading in to Wewak for the weekend there visiting staff.

A large group of men from the community had gathered in the open air church building and I joined them. The meeting proceeded smoothly. Kathy meanwhile had just quietly joined the women folk who were sitting on the grass under shade trees, making their *bilums*. Pulling out her latest cross-stitch sampler, she just made herself at home among them. I must admit I had not even wondered where she was, so focused was I on the meeting! But everyone else present knew exactly where she was - sitting with their women.

Once the meeting had finished and I was walking out with some of the men, I asked where Kathy was, and was advised she was with the other women. Then I heard a comment from someone behind me, talking to another person, *"Em i meri bilong PNG"* (She is a PNG woman).

It was one of those times when the truth began to sink in and I realised that any relational credibility I had was probably due much more to her than any claim I could make! The community had been impressed by the way she built a relationship with them just by quietly joining them and being with them. It was not what she did, but who she was.

As Christians committed to a ministry of sharing the gospel of Christ in PNG, all staff join with local churches. Many of our local staff are also leaders in their own local churches. For international missionary staff, we introduce them to churches in the area they are living in. Some of the outstation bases are under the umbrella of a single denomination, whereas in the towns, multiple denominations have thrived. Early in the history of missions in PNG, a comity arrangement was struck between denominations and inter-denominational missionary organisations which allocated regions or geographical areas to each group to evangelise. In more modern times, the rise of more diverse churches and denominations has meant that there is competition for souls all across PNG.

Our own church affiliation was with the Evangelical Church of PNG (ECPNG), a national denomination since 1966, spread across the Southern Highlands and Western Province, as well as a presence in towns outside those provinces, such as Mt Hagen and Port Moresby. Between 1987 and 1991 Kathy and I had worked exclusively as missionaries with this church with a focus of developing leaders through discipleship training. The church had ordained me as a Pastor in 1991. So we already had a strong history with a local church.

We sought ways that we could encourage new international staff in learning Tok Pisin (Pidgin English) and feeling more at home in PNG. I was invited to open a new ECPNG church building at Erave in the Southern Highlands. On a good day it is only about a 30 minute flight south of Mt Hagen in a light aircraft, landing on the grass airstrip. We invited a new (pilot) couple from Canada, Dave and Robyn, to join us for the weekend at Erave. However, we needed to drive down, so we loaded up the Hilux 4WD twin cab and set off. The road was atrocious, whether on the bitumen 'highlands highway' that started the trip, or on the rough limestone surface that followed. The return trip, covering 275km, took over 11 hours of driving! It was a good reminder of the value of flying.

The church opening was a huge celebration and deep trenches were dug in the ground to cook the dozens of pigs which were killed and cut up into the ground ovens *(mumu)*. Wrapped in banana leaves, they would be covered in hot rocks and allowed to steam cook for several hours. Chickens, root vegetables, bananas and greens would be included. I recall one conversation with an old man who proudly told me that the huge pig beside him was going to be slaughtered for this mumu.

I invited Dave to join me playing guitar during the church service, introducing him to the spontaneity of ministry in Melanesia! They later commented that the weekend had been so helpful for them because they had felt a bit restricted in what they could see and do in Mt Hagen since arriving. This experience had given them a fresh perspective on life in PNG.

In 2006 the ECPNG leaders invited me to speak at their annual General Conference in September at Tari, their headquarters. This was a time of fellowship for leaders from across the provinces, as well as learning from Scripture. I was honoured to be asked to speak. The topic assigned to me was False Cults. Across PNG a number of cults, from major 'denominational' based religions to home grown efforts, are finding fertile ground among established church members. Three areas of concern were mentioned - a Prosperity Movement (cargo cult) in one area; a dominance of focus on Israel in another; and in another area, a 'holiness' movement that forbade married women from sleeping with their husbands, with its negative implications socially!

I didn't feel that speaking against specific cultish groups would be to advantage. I wanted to be positive about genuine behaviour rooted in Godly worship. So I sought to highlight cultish behaviour and orthodox behaviour from the Scriptures. King Ahaz in the book of 2 Kings provides such an example of cultish behaviour, while his son Hezekiah, in the main, provides an example of true godly behaviour. My point was to say, recognise what cults look like and this is the alternative, godly practice based on a true understanding and worship of God.

I had found earlier that a teaching approach that focused on discovery learning in small groups was a most successful contextual approach to teaching in PNG. So I sought to apply this to the final of my sessions at the conference. Breaking them up into small groups of six or eight, I provided them the guidelines to conduct an inductive Bible study on the topic, where they sought to discover what Scripture was saying, and apply it to their context.

At the end of that session, as I walked away from the meeting hall, a school teacher came up to me and thanked me for the study.

"I have been a Christian for twenty years and read my Bible every day, but never really understood it. But tonight you gave me the keys to understand the Bible," he told me.

It reinforced for me the value in teaching people how to read and understand the Bible for themself through inductive study rather than just telling them what the Bible says, or even worse, reading the words without comprehending their meaning. The Bible is not a good luck charm or talisman. It is meant to be read so that we can understand the nature of God and salvation life in Christ.

Typical highlands bush airstrip, cut from the jungle on a hillside.

Pig feast *(mumu)* at Erave, SHP, for church opening.

14. WHEN TRUST IS BROKEN

Every now and then though that relationship of trust would be broken. One Traffic Officer decided to add an extra '1' to the amount listed on a cheque – at the beginning of the amount! – before cashing it in. He was stood down. His father worked in an aviation role with another organisation at the Mt Hagen airport. Soon after, the father arranged to see me in my office, with his son. He was angry that his son had been terminated and expressed that clearly to me. He wanted the son reinstated. I listened to him before letting him know that his son had one chance and had made his own decision in the matter. Theft and fraud were not tolerated. The father was not happy, but I encouraged the son to move on from MAF and find a new opportunity, having learnt from his MAF experience. As the discussion concluded, I said I would like to pray for the son. So we bowed our heads and I prayed for them and for the son's future. When I looked up again, the father's demeanour had changed. With a smile on his face, he thanked me, shook my hand and they left the office.

In another case, a Traffic Officer was discovered to have been siphoning off money from ticket sales for some time. When confronted, he stated that he was doing it to sponsor a relative through Bible College! The age-old question - does the end justify the means?

While there were unfortunately several instances of theft that we had to deal with, it was the lack of trust in staff maintaining safety procedures that was most challenging. In one case, an aircraft was refuelled with the wrong fuel type. Empty aviation fuel drums had been filled with vehicle diesel fuel ready to ship to another port. The traffic officer concerned had, contrary to standard procedures, not marked on the drums that they were now filled with diesel, then parked the drums on the tarmac near where the aviation fuel drums were stored. Soon after, when he was on a day off, the other traffic officers used the drums to refuel an aircraft without realizing it was not aviation fuel. The aircraft took off and the error was not discovered until next day when the traffic officer, back on duty, prepared to consign the drums and realised the fuel had been used, so he reported it.

Fortunately the turbine powered Twin Otter aircraft was able to operate okay on the diesel for a short time without repercussions and steps were taken to ensure there was no further contamination. Had it been a piston engined aircraft, the engine would have quit very quickly, with the disastrous possibility of an engine failure during take off. As we discussed the situation at Leadership Team, my response was that the matter was such a serious breach of standard procedures and common sense that the traffic officer should be terminated for his incompetence. While some had reservations, I followed through to terminate him.

MAF has a stated policy that the organisation will not take disciplinary action against an employee who self-reports a safety issue. This was part of a growing implementation of a 'Just Culture' framework throughout the aviation industry which found its origins in early accident investigation, which tended to blame the pilot without really considering further contextual issues. While I felt that the matter was of such recklessness on the part of the traffic officer that it warranted dismissal, senior managers in MAF Australia intervened, concerned that we uphold the reporting policy, and that, as the traffic officer had made the disclosure himself, he should not be terminated. He was subsequently reinstated.

One of the challenges in a serious and potentially disastrous case like this is determining the level of culpability in the person's action and how the policy should be applied when considering the incident in more detail. For example, should someone who deliberately creates an unsafe situation (which could be regarded as recklessness or even sabotage), then self-reports it, be able to claim immunity under this policy?

A few years after completing my term as General Manager, I was able to find an answer to this question. At a seminar on aviation safety conducted with major airline representatives by Air Services Australia, I was introduced to research that further defined culpability and responsibility. The research was applied through a flow chart which posed questions such as:

- *Did the person do this deliberately? (Y/N)*
- *Did they knowingly flout the rules or procedures? (Y/N)*
- *Were there other ways it could have been done? (Y/N)*
- *Was the person's motivation doing it for company or personal gain? (Y/N)*

The flow chart led to four main outcomes: *error, mistake, recklessness* and *sabotage,* each with rising culpability. A line in the sand was drawn between the first two and the second two, based around the person's intentionality and the consequences. The first two then are unintentional in nature and therefore handled by counselling and retraining, which are non-disciplinary in nature. For the second two, recklessness and sabotage, the action is deemed to be intentional, whether the negative outcome was desired or not, and is handled by management at a disciplinary level, up to termination, and may even be subject to legal sanction.

This model has continued to develop the Just Culture framework by expanding the understanding of intentionality and culpability, so that more modern organisational Safety Policies now include their self-reporting policy within that framework. I subsequently found that applying this model to situations provided a much more comprehensive approach to understanding a management response to incidents. This is much fairer for the person involved, as it takes their circumstances and motivation into full account yet maintains assessment within a defined structure. I wish I had seen that research and model much earlier. It would have made decision making much less stressful, including a fuller analysis of the Twin Otter refuelling incident.

Ochre face, Wobegon.
(from original watercolour)

15. MISSIONARY CHALLENGES

Papua New Guineans are beautiful people and most expatriates to PNG are captured by this beauty. One young international volunteer to MAF PNG found himself enamoured with one of our delightful local female staff members and commenced a relationship with her based on his own cultural norms, such as holding hands in public. Unfortunately it was inappropriate, both for him to start such a relationship but also to not understand the cultural norms within this society of which he was a visitor. I called them both in to discuss it with them, with the conclusion that the relationship needed to stop. While there was disappointment on both sides, they responded positively. The female staff member continued on to have a vital contribution in her MAF work for many years and the young man continued his role as a MAF volunteer and then returned back to his home country.

People often see cross cultural mission, such as we were engaged in, as being focused on the host culture. So there can be blind spots particularly in recognising that there are cultural differences between nationalities comprising the missionary team. With over 100 national staff and 50 or more international missionary staff, MAF PNG is a challenging environment. So dealing with the cultural diversity among the missionaries is challenging at times.

In the months immediately following the accident, recognising that communication with the team needed improvement, I started two communication initiatives. One was a monthly internal email newsletter. Called *'Generalisations On Selected Specific Informational Pieces'* ... (GOSSIP), it sought to update the team on anything and everything going on internally. It included Leadership Team decisions, people movements, events and anything else of interest to everyone. A little while later, one pilot told me that he observed that his wife relaxed noticeably once she received the email each month. So I realised it was being successful in communicating.

The second was a printed A4 MAF PNG Monthly Newsletter, mastheaded *'Flying Higher'*, which sought to communicate information about what was going on in MAF PNG for both internal readers and broader circulation to others interested. This contained a monthly prayer guide also, *'Partnering'*.

We also commenced a monthly staff recognition award, the *'Kumul Award'*, allowing people to nominate a fellow worker to receive the award, based on some action or response that was beyond their normal job description. Named after the national Bird of Paradise emblem, it expressed excellence in serving. Recipients also received a bonus in cash or kind as an incentive. It was always a joy to present these awards month by month though after a while we received fewer and fewer nominations. Recipients were acknowledged during a public awarding attended by staff, and in *'Flying Higher'*.

However there were still particular challenges that extended well beyond just information or reward.

When a new international family arrived (having spent some time in Australia en route) and were assigned a house on our compound, we invited them for dinner on their first night. We had visited their country twice a few years earlier teaching mission dynamics, loved their culture, and so looked forward to being with them and having them on the team. All was going well until halfway through the meal, when the wife became quite irate and distressed. She reacted to some aspects of MAF's policy regarding children's schooling. We were surprised by her reaction to say the least.

Over the next weeks and months, we saw more and more irrational behaviour from the wife, to the point where other families on the compound were apprehensive to even walk past her house. It increased to the extent that another senior family living next door were reconsidering their future in MAF because of the stress it was causing. The wife had also been very active in the local community and church but we saw that she was actually causing division in the community as well. It came to a head when I received a letter from the church stating that the church wanted no involvement with her – they were clearly distancing themselves from her!

Over the months I had raised this issue with MAF HQ management in Australia, who were rightly concerned that any drastic action may affect the broader relationship between MAF and the sending country involved. But it frustrated me to see the situation worsening without resolve. It was discovered also that the wife had somehow evaded some of the normal orientation program that all candidates participate in, and so evaluation of their application had not been complete. Finally it was decided to ask the family to return to Australia to complete orientation, or conclude their service with MAF in PNG. They chose the latter and left MAF to pursue their goals elsewhere in PNG independently. We were sorry to lose her husband's good contribution to the ministry though.

The process to become a fully-fledged pilot with MAF in PNG is time consuming. There are months of initial orientation both to the culture and flying. Pilots generally start flying as a co-pilot on the Twin Otter under a training Captain. Once they achieve the competencies required, they are approved as a Co-pilot and can fly with regular Captains. After gaining more experience, they will graduate to single pilot operations on the C206 or GA8. It takes four or five years before a pilot graduates to flying the Twin Otter as a Captain.

At every step of the way, the trainee co-pilot is mentored and encouraged as their bush flying skills develop. At our Leadership Team meetings we regularly review their progress. Unfortunately when a pilot struggles more than anticipated and is unable to attain the skill level required, we have to truthfully assess them as not being able to progress past training, and release them. This happened a couple of times. It was difficult to have to advise a pilot, who had spent years to get to this point in time, that he could no longer continue on flying with us. This is not just a management decision, it is a spiritual decision because we are intervening in their life and calling to this ministry. So it is made prayerfully recognising that we are, in effect, determining what God's will for them is at this point in time.

Two pilots who we took off flying like this went on to have successful ministries in other countries and organisations, for which we are thankful. A third situation was more complicated. For months the training Captain, Richard, had reviewed the pilot's progress with the Leadership Team as he sought opportunity to develop the pilot's skills-set to reach the required standard. But their probation period was expiring. Then I received reports of problems at their residential compound. Once again the wife was reported as exhibiting attitudes which were disruptive on the compound, to the extent that it was negatively affecting the other families. Unfortunately no one had advised me of this situation earlier on and so it had degenerated to become serious.

The combination left me no choice but to meet with them, together with the Chief Pilot, and advise them that we were releasing them. The couple reacted poorly unfortunately. I was not popular and in the months ahead was probably the target of some angst, including in their home country!

Unfortunately, as a manager you are sometimes dealing with the negatives in a few people's behaviour or circumstances. What one must remember is that the vast majority of co-workers are dedicated and astute people, committed to active Christian discipleship, and prayerfully making awesome contributions to the ministry and fellowship.

Despite that, I found it very difficult when I became aware that a staff member was actively unsupportive. One way this happened was by witholding information about matters that should have been communicated to the Leadership Team. When a member of the missionary team became over stressed, lost his cool and lashed out physically, damaging property, the immediate missionary families closest rightly sought to support him and his wife, but without disclosing it. I was very concerned to find out about it some time later. We had a tense discussion on duty of care responsibilities, which I believed obliged them to report it to management rather than try and just deal with it themselves in isolation. Not only did I need to know about this to continue to assess his fitness for his role in the team, but needed to ensure we could assist him and his family members at whatever level was needed.

On another occasion a co-worker came to me saying, "My wife suggested I should try working with you rather than against you." It was the start of a much better relationship with mutual respect for each other. I appreciated his wife's counsel so much, and his willingness to humble himself this way and make a new start.

There was a growing awareness of the need to do more in finding resources to assist our field staff. Once or twice a year, MAF Australia would arrange for some counsellors to visit PNG and spend some time with individual families. Alan and Meg Roberts took up this role and their visits were appreciated. It gave people a chance to confidentially unload their experiences. While fully supportive of this, I did have a concern that while people could openly vent their problems, the counsellors had no power or authority to change anything as they were independent of management. There was, deliberately, no communication of confidential issues by the counsellors to management, which is the basis for confidential counselling. So in areas where the Leadership Team may have been able to implement changes to address staff concerns, there was very limited ability to do so if we were not made aware of them.

There were inspirational events which brought us great encouragement. In the 27 years since Dean's father Jim's accident high in the Torricelli Mountains of the Sepik Province, the aircraft position had been lost to the rest of the world as the jungle enfolded it into obscurity. GPS positioning had not been available in 1979 and once the accident investigation team had finished, the only reference was, "about 18km south-west of Aitape". One of Dean's ambitions while in PNG was to discover again the accident site - and perhaps visit it. He had already been able to visit his father's grave site and plaque in Wewak.

The best information he could garner came from local villagers who claimed some of the students walking to school across the ranges had reported seeing wreckage. So in May 2006, Dean and fellow MAF pilot Chris arranged a journey by motorbike and foot up into the identified area, spending two nights camping in a nearby village. Dean has written of this experience himself, how villagers along the way helped to carry the motorbikes across rivers or free them when bogged, experiences of miraculous intervention for Dean.

When they arrived at the location, writes Dean, "Exploring the crash site was a surreal experience. It was the confluence of a whole range of thoughts and emotions. Here I was, standing at the last place my father had been alive. I also reflected and grieved over the families that were in that aircraft." A missionary family of five had also died in the crash.

Dean found some parts of the aircraft still identifiable in the undergrowth and was able to commandeer a damaged propeller blade in remembrance. We all found Dean's journey to find his father's lost aircraft inspirational, acknowleging the emotional impact for him as he found decades old questions answered, and new ones raised in his own spiritual journey.

In 2004, on the 25th anniversary of that accident, a long term missionary in the Sepik who had been involved in the accident events wrote to Dean, stating that, "I strongly believe that the event brought a spiritual breakthrough in the Aitape area and today there are 28 [of our] churches in the area, as well as many others." Once again, this mystery of the recognition of divine impact through human tragedy.

Each morning staff would gather at their work locations for a devotional time of worship and challenge from Scripture. After the MFQ accident we sought initiatives which would enhance our corporate fellowship. While people were attending a church of their choosing on Sunday mornings, we initiated a Sunday evening service in Mt Hagen specifically for all MAF staff there. Held in a large hired room at the Highlander Hotel, and called *'Soulfood'*, various staff members brought their gifts and skills in music and preaching or teaching, as well as hospitality, to a family friendly gathering. An added bonus was the Highlander's pool and pizza bar, enabling families to enjoy some relaxation before the service. I hope it had another bonus as well. Most people who are new to a foreign culture find that church in another language doesn't really "do much" for them. So the opportunity to sing familiar Christian songs and relate in a familiar language can be very helpful as people adjust to a new cultural context.

Annual Staff Conference was already a regular fixture on the MAF PNG calendar, usually soon after mid year. All missionary staff would gather for up to five days for fellowship and spiritual encouragement, with a visiting speaker, and training and refresher opportunities for technical issues.

Given the nature of the events at start of the year, we decided to make the 2005 mid-July Conference a joint event, with missionary and local staff all together. Our national staff usually had their own Conference at a different time. As no other speaker had been arranged in time, our friends Ray and Di Budge, working with another mission, SSEM, in the Sepik, accepted our invitation to come. Held in Mt Hagen at the Mt Hagen International School, with people once again billeted out with Hagen based families, the theme was "Blessed be the Name of the Lord". Ray led studies in the book of Ruth, with lots of opportunity for group discussion and practical expression allowing us to explore a deeper sense of purpose in this ministry. It provided a great way to extend the relationships between our missionary and local staff. A number of awards were given out to staff - Kathy received the 'GMM Award - General Manager's Manager Award', recognition of her work behind the scenes supporting me!

In 2006 and 2007, a pastor team from north Qld, Phil and Julie Bignall, presented the teaching sessions. Phil's fitting theme for 2006 was 'Rebuilding our walls, Renewing our strength, Restoring our souls'. In the Conference a huge blow-up photo of P2-MFT on corflute was cut into small brick sized sections. During the Conference we were invited to write our prayer requests on the back of a brick, which was then placed back into its position. It was a fitting reminder of the spiritual nature of our work, the hidden factor behind MFT.

These annual conferences continued to play a vital role in getting everyone together, bearing in mind that this may be the only chance some of them, especially the wives, caught up with each other, being scattered across six or seven bases.

Dean at his father's grave site in Wewak.

Conference 2005 discussion.

Local village level church near Mt Hagen.

16. P2-MFJ

At a purely business operational level, we struggled with the cost of operating and maintaining a fleet of aircraft in an inhospitable environment, even if the purpose was honourable. So discussion about how to keep airfares for the missionaries, church workers and general travelling public at a minimum was often in our Leadership Team discussions. Already MAF PNG had implemented a graded airfare structure that enabled church and missionary personnel to travel at greatly discounted rates. One of the pilots, Pierre, had been instrumental in developing this policy and, in his respected role as Church & Missions Coordinator, had spent much time and effort in liaison with the various church and missions agencies who we served. Travel by missionary and church personnel accounted for just over 10% of passengers in 2004, with discounts up to 80% offered depending the person's role and reason for travel, with Bible school students and pastors having the highest priority.

But was there a way to reduce costs for the general public without reducing our fares based income so needed to maintain financial viability?

Realising that we needed to extend our contacts in the PNG capital, I elected to make regular, at times monthly, trips to engage face to face with various officials from government departments and other relevant organisations in Port Moresby. This included meeting with senior people from the Civil

Aviation Authority (CAA), Finance or Treasury, Planning, Members of Parliament, provincial Governors and others for whom we needed to have contact. It was a great help having Vaughan to work together in this as he had already established many contacts in his role in Government liaison with MAF PNG.

Maintaining relationships with the CAA was critical. We operated under their rules and were subject to regular auditing to ensure standards were maintained. One of their requirements was that the most senior accountable person in an aviation organisation receives a 'Senior Person' approval. So it was that on one of my first visits to Port Moresby on 22nd March, 2005, I successfully undertook my Senior Person's interview with Wilson Sagati, the current Director.

During this visit to the capital we also approached the Internal Revenue Commission (IRC - responsible for taxation and customs) to consider exempting MAF from payment of VAT (Value Added Tax/GST) on the basis that this would substantiate the 'community service obligation' (cso) to rural communities enshrined in government legislation. We knew that there were similar schemes operating for mining companies, for example.

In the mid 1980's, while Kathy and I were stationed in Port Moresby with MAF, we met a young lawyer, who also was a mean guitarist, at the church we attended. He began working with the IRC in Customs. Twenty years later, David Sode was now the IRC Commissioner and also a member of the MAF PNG Board. His advice was that there was no legal basis for IRC to offer VAT exemption. So we realised we would have to pursue other avenues with government.

One possibility that emerged was to enter into an agreement with a Provincial Government, who administered expenses in their province, so that they covered a portion of airfare costs on behalf of their people. Late in 2005 I raised the matter with the Governor of the Western Province, Dr Bob Danaya, who invited me down to address their Provincial Assembly in Daru. The result, in time, was an agreement that the provincial government would allocate an amount of funds to MAF PNG, while MAF in turn would discount all airfares for travel within the province by the agreed percentage, until the grant was used up for that time period. The discount only applied to flights wholly within the Western Province. Our accountant was able to figure out a way to facilitate this with the paperwork and flight manifests, and for a period of a year or more, travellers benefited from the discount.

The theory was that if airfares are cheaper, more people will travel, so the benefit for MAF would be more airfares, so increased revenue (normally achieved by increasing airfare values!). The disadvantage was in the increased administration time and costs, and in review, no financial advantage if there was not an uptake in travel. In the end I don't think we saw any real change in the number of people travelling – the cost of airfares was still well out of the reach of most people.

Another more significant outcome did come from my meetings with Dr Danaya. MAF has traditionally funded the purchase of new aircraft from donations. The Governor liked the idea of sponsoring the cost of an aircraft for use in the Western Province, particularly to be stationed at our Rumginae base, serving the Rumginae Health Centre. Pilots regularly reported several medevac flights a week bringing patients into Rumginae. Snake bites, maternal health issues, childbirth, and accidents, all provided an opportunity of hope for those flown in to the mission doctors at Rumginae Health Centre, which also ran a nurse training school.

The Governor committed to the cost of purchasing an Airvan GA8, the new type which was being introduced into the MAF PNG operation. In consultation with our MAF HQ leadership, we believed his commitment was genuine and so made the decision to order an aircraft from the factory in Gippsland, Victoria. In a number of subsequent calls with the Governor, he reiterated his commitment to the project and said he had submitted the appropriate funding request.

As the months rolled on and the aircraft began to be assembled in the factory, two critical aspects emerged. The first was that a date was set by the factory to receive the funding required to purchase the aircraft, or it would be allocated to the next customer order in line. MAF didn't want to miss this opportunity to add to its aircraft fleet. The second was that this aircraft was to be the 100th GA8 to come off the assembly line and would therefore be the subject of more fanfare than is normal. This would also give MAF an opportunity to benefit from the promotional aspects which would ensue.

Despite the Governor's assurances, with little more than two or three weeks until deadline, it became clear that the Governor's funding source had not eventuated. I discovered later that his application had been in conjunction with that for a coastal vessel and there had been complications, though the coastal vessel did eventually become a reality, bearing his name.

PNG Sustainable Development Program (PNGSDP) originated from the Ok Tedi mine legislation as a way to receive and distribute royalties from the mine equitably, primarily but not exclusively within the Western Province. The CEO, Mr Robert Igara, had attended the same boarding school as me in Australia in the 1960's, though I had not known him well. However he warmed to the idea of sponsoring the cost of the aircraft at short notice, and its mission role at Rumginae as sitting well within the SDP mandate. Two weeks later a cheque for two million kina (about AU$800,000) was in my hands, and with a sigh of relief we were able to advise the factory that our order was genuine!

Some months later, on August 23rd, 2006, when the aircraft was ready for delivery, Kathy and I attended the ceremony at the factory in Gippsland, Victoria, to welcome the aircraft into the real world. The (Australian) Minister for Transport gave a speech and the work of MAF was spoken of, recognising that MAF was already operating several GA8 aircraft in Arnhem Land. The aircraft was taken on an aerial tour of a number of towns on its way up to PNG, stopping off to showcase it to friends and supporters along the way. Once in PNG it was registered as P2-MFJ and commissioned to the Rumginae base.

There was some political fallout from these events. The Governor called me when the SDP deal had been finalised and was not happy at all about this change in sponsorship. I could only advise him that his promised funding had not been forthcoming in time and welfare opportunities for the people of the Western Province were at stake. Both the Provincial Government and SDP receive royalties from the Ok Tedi mine and so there are some political challenges involved in the matter of project sponsorship. A key person behind the scenes in SDP was Mr Ati Wobira, who had been very involved in seeing the GA8 project come to fruition. Mr Wobira later stood against Dr Danaya in the provincial elections and won, to become the new Governor of Western Province. Both men were also members of the ECPNG church denomination that we had significant ties to, and I counted them as friends. It was a shame that the events created a distance between Dr Danaya and myself.

Once MFJ arrived in Rumginae, a dedication was held in the parking bay on 3rd February 2007, with SDP Board member Sir Ebia Olewale handing over the keys as the aircraft was commissioned with the blessings of the church, mission and health centre. It was particularly fulfilling to have the CEO comment to me that he felt this had been the best investment SDP had made that year. An added bonus came soon after when an MAF Australian manager advised me I was also their most successful fund-raiser!!

Dr Bob Danaya, Western Province Governor, presents the first payment for airfare subsidies in the Western Province to me.

Receiving the cheque for K2m from PNGSDP CEO, Mr Robert Igara (ctr), and Board member, Sir Ebia Olewale (from newspaper story).

P2-MFJ decorated in flowers ready for the commissioning

Bill Harding (MAF CEO) receives the aircraft keys from Sir Ebia Olewale, PNGSDP Board member.

MAF PNG Board, church and local leaders prayer of dedication.

P2-MFJ (ironically the same registration as on my commissioning cake).

Home made GA8 at Rumginae.

Parking bay at Kawito on a busy day.

17. P2-MFO and P2-MFP

Aircraft are subject to continual maintenance and checking to ensure they are able to continue operating safely for many years. The regular 100 hourly inspection (after 4-6 weeks of flying usually) takes a good look over the aircraft, carries out engine and airframe maintenance, and replaces various parts that may be worn or time expired. At the other end of the maintenance schedule is the major overhaul, known more recently as a C Check. This can take weeks and even months to complete and is basically a complete and thorough overhaul of the aircraft, often including repaint.

A Cessna 206, with damage sustained during a landing incident, was purchased from another operator and entered its major overhaul/repair in the Mt Hagen hangar during 2005. One of the aircraft engineers, Brad, was assigned to complete the job. Known for his excellence in workmanship, he spent several months working away at the overhaul, resulting in a magnificent aircraft that looked virtually new. When I knew that the aircraft was ready to re-enter service, we planned to have a dedication service around the aircraft to commission it into service again.

In the few days prior to the commissioning, I considered what words I should say at the event, words that would encourage the staff, recognising that it was just over a year since the Twin Otter accident. I believe that God very firmly impressed a particular verse upon me to share, but for the life of me I could not find where it was in the Bible! Finally on the night before the dedication, I discovered it.

Psalm 139:7-10 (NIV):

Where can I go from your Spirit?

Where can I flee from your presence?

If I go up to the heavens, you are there;

If I make my bed in the depth, you are there.

If I rise on the wings of the dawn,

If I settle on the far side of the sea,

Even there your hand will guide me,

Your right hand will hold me fast.

As we commenced our day's work with the aircraft dedication, I shared the message that as this aircraft flies around the country, carrying the pilots, missionaries and church people, and those from the community, none can flee from God. He is always with them, up in the clouds or down in the valleys, God's hand will guide and his right hand will hold them firmly in his grip.

All our Mt Hagen team joined hands in a circle around the aircraft in the hangar and joyfully commissioned this tool for God's purposes, registered now as P2-MFO, before it was rolled out onto the tarmac ready to fly. It was March 23rd, 2006.

Little more than two hours later, I received the message that another of our aircraft had crashed. Cessna 206 P2-MFP, a sister aircraft to MFO, had crashed short of the airstrip following a power loss while approaching to land at Tari in the Southern Highlands, later Hela Province.

I gathered the leaders together again as an Emergency Response Team. We began to understand more of what had happened as more details came in, once again by HF radio from those at the scene. Another pilot had been able to land at Tari soon after and get down to the stricken aircraft, and we awaited his report.

We were struggling. How could this happen so soon after the earlier accident? Have we lost another pilot so tragically?

The Swiss pilot, Pierre Fasnacht, had three passengers on board and was based in Mt Hagen, so we needed to inform his wife, Esther as soon as we could. Because the airport is 14km from Mt Hagen town, I asked Kathy, who was in town, to go with the Chief Pilot's wife, Christina, to let Esther immediately know of the accident situation. Christina (who was also among Esther's closest friends) was not at home when I called her, so Kathy went by herself. As soon as Esther opened the front door to Kathy, she knew something was wrong. Christina came soon after, and other MAF people arrived to provide support for Esther and her four children.

Once the pilot at the crash scene was able to reach a phone again, he confirmed that Pierre had died on impact. The three passengers, sitting in the middle seats, had survived but some injuries were evident. We were grief stricken once again.

The Emergency Response Team continued to liaise with follow up agencies and a helicopter company provided a helicopter to fly the injured passengers to a mission run hospital at Kudjip near Mt Hagen. Once again we never received a bill for the flight.

The most heart-wrenching part for me was to follow. Thirteen months earlier we had gathered at the terminal as the families and support team taxied in and disembarked. This time as the aircraft from Tari taxied in, it was the pilot's body in a body bag that we unloaded. While sanitised scenes of white sheets over bodies are not infrequent in the movies or on TV now, the reality of unloading your workmate in a body bag is different. It is raw and shocking.

There is no real support infrastructure in PNG in situations like this, it is left to families or employing companies, and so we had to personally manage the need to care for his body. The Chief Pilot, Volkher, and I took him to the morgue in Mt Hagen, a refrigerated container which would have barely met any temperature controls. PNG was experiencing an HIV/AIDS epidemic and morgue space was at a premium. Crude wooden shelves about 40 cm apart in vertical spacing had been constructed on either side of the container and we found a vacant shelf among the sheet-covered bodies.

A few days later when Esther and her children were ready to view Pierre, Volkher and I lifted him back onto the bare steel table in the mortuary room in his body bag. I could not look into his face and kept to one side, I did not want to experience any more of this horror than we were already experiencing. Once zipped up, it was back onto the shelf again. There was something disrespectful and indignant about it, that his exemplary life was reduced to this shelf. But this was the only mortuary facility available.

Once again we brought all our missionary families into Mt Hagen and billeted them out with the Mt Hagen families. We reached out to another mission, SIL, which graciously sent some counsellors to help us through this time. MAF also facilitated an in-house couple to assist. Alan and Meg Roberts were previous MAF staff. Alan was a pilot and radio technician who had served as General Manger in MAF PNG previously. They now offered their time as counsellors and I was very glad to be able to assign Alan to debrief with the pilots. A joint MAF-EBC memorial service was held in Mt Hagen at the EBC church on 29th March, 2006. (The Fasnachts were also members of the Swiss Evangelical Brotherhood Church).

Much as we wished it had not happened, we recognised that Kathy and Esther had shared in the most difficult and traumatic of events in life. A few days later, for some reason, we felt it important to share with Esther the dedication of MFO earlier on the day of Pierre's accident in MFP, so we decided to visit her.

As I started to share with her about trying to find the Bible verse, Psalm 139, and then speaking on it, Esther looked at me and said, "Don't you know?" in her inimitable direct Swiss style.

I looked bewildered.

"Don't you know?" she asked again.

"No, what?" I replied.

"That was the Bible verse Pierre put on our prayer card," Esther said.

We were stunned! This was his verse, his promises that he claimed from God for his missionary service with MAF, rising up with wings to settle on the far side of the sea from his native Switzerland. We realised that he didn't crash into the ground, he crashed into the right hand of God.

It began to dawn on us that the dedication of MFO, as I spoke from Psalm 139, was actually more about MFP and Pierre, almost like the Lord reminded us of his promises to Pierre beforehand. Once again we recognised God's hand of grace and timing evident in midst of the heartache and pain.

It was decided by the family to repatriate Pierre's body back to Switzerland. Arrangements were made for temporary sealing of a coffin for his travel to Port Moresby, where full embalming would be done to enable his flight home. I had arranged for an ambulance to bring the coffin out to the airport freight terminal in preparation for the flight.

To ensure things went smoothly, I went to the hospital in good time, where I was unexpectedly advised that, "No, the ambulance is for living people, not dead people, so it can't be used."

I now had to find an alternative transport quickly by myself. I was using a small MAF van-mini bus so went straight to the morgue just around the corner. However, with the middle seats still installed in the van, the coffin didn't fit inside and was left hanging half out the back. I rushed home to get some tools and removed the seats before returning to the morgue. By now I had lost a significant amount of time and was running out of time to get the coffin to airport check-in. The coffin fitted in now but by the time I reached the airport, it was past the check-in time. This was turning into a nightmare experience for me. The possibility of not being able to get the coffin onto the aircraft to Port Moresby was very real, and had me experiencing considerable anxiety.

As I backed up to the cargo shed counter and got out of the van, I was assaulted by an horrific smell. I suspect an animal had died in the gutter there. I was overwhelmed by this sensory assault, the stench of death and decay, as I unloaded the coffin onto the weighing scales and sorted out the paperwork. Fortunately the incoming flight was delayed and so I was able to complete the consignment, leaving the coffin unceremoniously on a baggage trolley. Somehow God had intervened to resolve the situation!

I was exhausted in every sense of the word. To see Pierre's coffin on the airplane would bring closure for me to another difficult episode. But as I watched, the baggage trolleys were wheeled onto the tarmac where the coffin would sit in the sun until the inbound flight arrived, and it was loaded into the Fokker 70's below deck freight compartment.

Finally, the flight departed and we were able to relax a little. But the emotional stress had taken its toll.

Pierre's prayer card.

Brad with MFO after major inspection completed.

18. WORN OUT

The weeks and months following Pierre's accident were difficult for everyone. The hope for better things following the Twin Otter accident was giving way to despair. Following their time debriefing with team members, Alan and Meg summed it up to me, saying that people were weary, feeling overloaded now and wondering how to cope, looking for ways to make drastic changes which will address the overload issues. Pierre's contribution as a fellow missionary, pilot and Church & Mission Coordinator had been huge and he left a huge hole in people's hearts as well as the program.

As 2006 progressed beyond this time, I was very aware of the stresses people were experiencing but felt caught up in it myself, limited in what I could do. For the third time in little over a year we had brought everyone into Mt Hagen, billeted by the Mt Hagen families. One evening, during the week after the accident, I received a call from one of the missionary wives expressing that it was too much to handle, the burden placed on the Mt Hagen families was overloading them. I felt like I could only reply with what felt like clichéd assurances, but hoped that at least the opportunity for her to unload was helpful.

Other issues became apparent as the year progressed. What started as a couple of MAF wives providing lessons for missionary children in Mt Hagen Baptist Church in the 1970s, developed to become a fully fledged high school. Buildings were erected on land secured near the centre of the township, and for several decades Bamboo Heights High School provided international level education for MAF and missionary children from other mission organisations. Education for their children is always a critical issue for missionaries. If suitable educational opportunities are not available locally, the options are limited to sending children away to boarding school or leaving the field as a family to return to the home country. Neither of these options are palatable for many parents.

By 2005, the situation had changed and Bamboo Heights was now an open International School, taking in students from all walks of life. For Papua New Guineans, it opened up an opportunity for their children to gain an education at an international standard rather than the level provided at regular community schools. Difficulties in recruiting overseas teachers resulted in educational standards dropping to below that considered necessary for some missionary parents. MAF also had the challenge of families living in some of the outstation airstrip communities where they were totally isolated and home-schooling the only option.

It became clear early on in my time that we had an educational crisis which needed some solutions, and it was the parents who were struggling. Those in outstations embraced home-schooling but struggled with limited support. Those in the town were struggling with finding an acceptable level of education locally for their children. It was affecting families, especially the wives, who bore the most burden at home.

We called a meeting of families, attended especially by the mothers, to open up discussion about the situation and seek to find answers together. I put on my best community development hat, on the basis that we could work this through together as a unified group to find the best solutions. I was there to facilitate the discussion with a view to listening, learning and negotiating the best way forward for management to implement what the group wanted. I came with an open mind.

There was some frank discussion and it was very clear that the issue was very emotive for parents. Some were facing real struggles the way things were. At one point though, before we had reached any conclusions, one of the parents said to me, "So what are *you* going to do about it?"

But this was not my problem, it was our problem, and I felt that my attempts to approach from that perspective had failed.

"What do *you* want to do about it?" I replied, letting the group know that I would implement whatever solution they wanted.

After further discussion, the group agreed that recruiting a teacher to provide support for parents, both in Mt Hagen, where the teacher would be based, and in the outstations, would be the best step forward. The Leadership Team immediately set that in process with the overseas Head Office and recruitment began, covered by prayer.

It was such a blessing when Rachel, a single woman teacher in Sydney, applied and was accepted for the position, commencing a few months later. I hoped that the result demonstrated my desire as the manager to seriously work with our team to find solutions. Rachel fitted in really well very quickly and was able to build good and positive relationships with the parents and children, and so meet the very real needs they had both in the towns and outstations.

We had started 2006 already in a dire situation with a pilot shortage - nine pilots short of the number needed to meet current operational demands, and recruitment slowing down. Engineers were also at minimum numbers. The fleet was one single engine aircraft down on optimum following a write-off accident in the Sepik (with no injuries), and now we were down another aircraft and pilot. Financially MAF PNG was needing to be propped up more and more from overseas, the loss of aircraft and their earning capacity a major factor affecting financial viability.

Working closely with MAF Australia leaders, the Leadership Team commenced a peer process to seriously look at changes needed in the program, to be presented to the Board in late May. After consultation with all staff, the 'Change Team' identified 15 themes from which recommendations for change would follow:

- Cultural Awareness;
- Identity (vision, purpose, values, mission);
- Training;
- Staffing (including performance reviews);
- Structure & management;
- Operations (including staff mentoring and management);
- Communications;
- Types of Work (key customers and high value);
- Staff support & sustainability;
- Rationalisation of bases;
- Prayer;
- PNG partnerships;
- Aircraft types & models of operation; and
- Engineering.

Ongoing meetings would continue to elicit staff feedback and provide direction for positive change. Much as local initiatives such as reducing bases would help, the heart of the problem was under-resourcing of the program with the people needed - pilots, engineers and managers. With more people on the field, operating revenue increases as flying hours increase, the need for more aircraft then follows, and the workload is spread. And most importantly, we are able to achieve more in terms of our purpose of supporting physical and spiritual transformation in remote communities. As the new partnership of individual MAF organisations worldwide drew closer to becoming a reality, our hope was that MAF International would boost recruitment and provide the needed support.

Kathy and I needed to get a break. As Easter came, we spent five days at a Swiss missionary retreat house at Kugark, 30 minutes drive from Mt Hagen. It was a beautiful, quiet place, part of a small missionary outpost, looking out over the Waghi Valley to the north, and majestic mountain ranges to the south.

We went for walks, including one day up into the mountains in company with several local people we had met. The base of the Waghi Valley is around 5,000' above sea level. I estimated we reached at least 7,000' following well worn paths in kunai grass up the mountain side. Passing through a small village, our guide pointed out the numerous grave sites around the village. HIV/AIDS was claiming a huge toll in lives lost, so tragic. We went as far as we could easily manage, finding an old man living alone in his grass roofed hut. Family members would come regularly to bring him food and keep an eye on him. His view was spectacular. I could understand why he preferred the solitude of his mountain hut to the pressures of life further down the mountainside!

For the five days I could not sleep. I tried to express my feelings by doing a painting. It started out as a jumble of shapes, straight sharp edges, not smooth. Sharp points emerged, like pointed nails. Pieces of rough timber started to become visible, as other shapes swirled around. Colours found their way onto the watercolour paper, the purple of a robe, a maroon cushion fit for a king's chair, some blue sky and nondescript pale shades. It represented the jumble and confusion I was feeling, so I aptly titled it, 'Easter Confusion'. And then across the shapes, the nails, the wood and the robe, something else emerged. A white bird, a dove, flying across the page, over all the confusion.

Painting a picture is not going to miraculously deliver someone from the emotional reality of an intense and difficult time, but it did give me an opportunity to express something that was otherwise inexpressible. I look back on it now, not as an amazing abstract or work of art, but as a genuine reaching out beyond myself in some sort of identification with all the elements of Christ that the painting exhibited. It helped.

It was during this time that I also did a painting depicting MFP in the Tari valley, backdropped by the Tari Gap, flying into the right hand of God. It was copied and sent round to our staff and workers as a way of reinforcing God's promises to Pierre in Psalm 139, encouraging them to see beyond the tragedy. I would still see that painting up on noticeboards years later.

In July 2006 we took our due bi-annual furlough back to Australia to get some R&R. During this trip I visited Melbourne and spent time with the senior clinical psychologist for State Emergency Services in Victoria, to learn of their trauma counselling program. It helped me better understand some of the dynamics involved and promote a more rigorous approach to this need within MAF. I went as far as joining the Critical Incident Stress Management Foundation Australia Inc. and in October attended a course titled 'Establishing and Maintaining a CISM Program in the Workplace'. My intention was to see how we could start to implement a more effective response on the field. Over the next few months I had a number of discussions about this need with MAF Australia HR and hope that it was helpful as they continued to address the issue on a broader scale. Certainly the training was a help to me personally as well, recognising my own stress, both personally and as a manager.

Returning to PNG two months later though, I found that little had changed and my sleeping patterns were erratic still. I was finding myself more and more under-confident in my ability to lead the mission. I was going through the motions at work but my heart wasn't always in it. By mid 2007 I had put up my hand to MAFI leadership and expressed my struggles. While there was little that they could do immediately, they did pledge to relieve me by mid 2008, whether there was a replacement for me or not.

Old man who lived in the mountains behind Kugark, WHP.

(from original watercolour)

'Into the Right Hand of God'
(from original watercolour)

'Easter Confusion'
(from original watercolour)

19. FLIGHT TRAINING SCHOOL

In the decade leading up to 2000, the MAF flight training centre in Mt Hagen had successfully trained at least 30 Papua New Guinean pilots to Commercial Licence. Some of them stayed on to become valued pilots with MAF while others worked with other aviation operators within PNG. Over time several became senior leaders in their airline or industry representation. MAF has made a vital contribution to the aviation industry at large in PNG, with MAF trained people held in high regard, even actively recruited.

By 2004 however the flying school had ceased to operate. For various reasons, including financial, the emphasis on pilot training had taken a back seat to flight operations, though training of engineering apprentices had continued. I considered training as a vital aspect of our MAF work in PNG though and so sought to revitalise pilot training. This was particularly relevant because the last of our PNG pilots resigned soon after and we were once again totally dependent on overseas pilot recruitment.

We were fortunate to have some key missionary engineering staff who were very committed to training in the engineering department. A steady stream of apprentices were working their way up to becoming Aircraft Maintenance Engineers (AME) and Licensed Aircraft Maintenance Engineers (LAME), mentored by trainer Brenton and supported by senior Engineer

Larry. Our Chief Engineer, Ben Agerenga from Chimbu Province, and future hangar supervisor, John Kamalan from New Ireland, were both appreciated and valued for their expertise. But we had dropped the ball on pilot training.

We already had both CAA licensing to run a flight school and a qualified and experienced Flight Instructor, Clint, in our team of pilots. What we did not have was an aircraft or the rubber stamp from MAF leadership to reopen the school.

I met with the MAF PNG Board quarterly and so my starting point was with them. The Board was made up of respected PNG leaders from various backgrounds, chaired by the MAF Australia Board Chairman. While operationally MAF PNG was an integral part of the emerging MAF International operation, the role of the Board was to provide oversight and direction for the PNG operation at policy level.

I presented the case for reopening the Flight Training Centre. The Board members were positive about this prospect and very supportive. The Chairman was hesitant and understood the history behind the closure, stemming I believe from decisions previously made by the MAF Australia Board. Concern over the financial drain the flight school could impose on the overall PNG operation, which was already needing substantial injections of donor funding to continue, was primary.

A broader discussion had focused on the value of our flight training program. Some saw it purely as a means to get more pilots into the MAF operation, and so if it did not meet that goal, it was not considered as viable. Others saw it as a valuable contribution to the nation of PNG, recognising not all will become MAF pilots. Our contribution was to the aviation industry as a whole, injecting in well trained professionals with influence as Christians.

The Board's conclusion was a decision to reopen the flight school as long as it ran financially independently of the main operation. I was very pleased with this decision as it opened the door once again to active engagement in pilot training.

Discipleship takes on many forms. I firmly believe that when we are empowering people, which is what training does, we are helping them to achieve their God-given potential. This is a reflection not only of our own desire to see God at work in others, but recognition of their potential, a potential for leadership at both a practical and spiritual level. Our flight training program sought to build good practical skills into disciples of Christ, providing positive input at both levels.

There was one major obstacle still. We did not have a training aircraft. The Cessna 206 aircraft which were the mainstay of our smaller aircraft fleet, were too sophisticated and expensive to use for training. Ideally a 2 or 4 seater aircraft was needed. As prayer went out for this need, we were thrilled when a European donor provided the funds to purchase a Cessna 172, regarded as the most suitable type for our training, from Australia.

Once the aircraft was in PNG and the school re-commenced in July 2006 under Clint as Chief Flying Instructor, the Board was able to participate in the dedication of the C172, registered as P2-MFA.[5]

---

5. The flight school continued successfully for some years and was eventually incorporated into the MAFI flight training facility in Mareeba, Australia.

MAF PNG Board members with P2-MFA.

Clint (left) with flight students and C172 aircraft.

20. PROVINCIAL CHALLENGES

While it may have seemed crazy to think of expanding bases to serve other provinces, we were being approached by leaders from around the country to serve their province too. I had leaders from a number of provinces contact me, including West New Britain, Bougainville and Milne Bay, as well as other mainland provinces.

The Milne Bay Governor, Tim Neville, had previously made contact and invited me to attend a meeting with the government's National Executive Council in Milne Bay in mid February, 2006. Tim had spent much of his life in the Southern Highlands where his family managed coffee plantations among other interests. He was a regular flyer with Paul Summerfield, who was based in Mendi at the time, and shared stories of some of his adventures flying with Paul.

The meeting would be held in Milne Bay, not in Alotau the provincial capital, but out on an island off the eastern tip of the mainland. Kos, our Ground Operations Manager, would come with me. We were driven the 20kms from Alotau in Landcruisers to the beach point at East Cape and then jumped into dingies for the 15 minute ride to Killerton Island. It was a return to Milne Bay for me. Between 1983 and 1986 I had flown weekly into the province from Port Moresby, where we were based with MAF, operating a Cessna 402C. Once again, my previous experience had provided familiarity with the area and people.

The meeting was what you could call 'Melanesian relaxed'! When we arrived we met some of the parliamentarians sitting on woven mats on the sand under the coconut trees.

Killerton Island is typical of small tropical islands that are basically coral banks with a grove of coconut trees and a few other bushes which have tolerated the salt water enough to grow. But it is a historical landmark in the history of PNG and the advent of Christian missionaries. It was on this small idyllic but inhospitable island that the first missionaries from the eastern Pacific came to evangelise PNG. They dug a hole to get water and constructed some buildings using coral and shells for their concrete walls, overgrown remnants of which remain today. It would have been very tough for them in the relentless tropical heat.

Fortunately our party today was not doing it so tough. Kos and I were able to interact with various government ministers in between them swimming in the pristine waters and enjoying fresh caught, barbecued red emperor fish, with bananas, sweet potato and yams! Even with this some were still unhappy - the dingies had forgotten to bring the eskies of beer from the shore! It didn't take long to discover a warm response to the ministry of MAF and indeed some substantial roots of identification with us by rural politicians.

As we walked a short way into the island, I was privileged to walk and talk with Dame Carol Kiru as we inspected the waterhole and overgrown ruins of a past era. I felt not only a sense of privilege to be stuck on a beer-less tropical island with the most senior politicians in PNG, but a deep sense of awe as we reflected on this momentous time in the spiritual history of PNG.

While meeting these top decision makers in PNG was largely informal in nature, it included the opportunity to discuss issues such as tax credits directly with the current Treasurer, Hon Bart Philemon, a previous Air Niugini CEO. He invited direct submissions to himself, acknowledging submissions by Vaughan the previous year were moving too slowly.

The next day Kos and I joined Governor Neville and senior provincial managers back in Alotau. The Governor was seeking to expand business opportunities in his province which provided direct benefit to the community. The province, we were told, was already the largest exporter of *beche de mer* (sea cucumber) into the world market, and also housed the only vanilla processing plant in the country. Several prospective large mine operations were in various stages of development. Coffee was also grown but in landlocked mountain valleys with no road access - the PNG Defence Force 'Green Revolution' initiative had shipped out 37 tons in their Arava aircraft the previous year. The main church denomination established in the province also had transport needs right through the province's network of islands.

Because the province covers such a large area, with much of it only accessible by ocean transport, the need for aircraft was critical. Ocean travel in small craft is expensive for outboard motor fuel costs, often dangerous in seasonal rough seas, and there is an increasing threat from pirate gangs, the marine equivalent of urban *raskol* gangs I guess! Even from nearby islands, a half hour flight by light aircraft could take 24 hours by boat. Outer islands were one to two hours flight time away or more. Unfortunately the only commercial operator providing regular light aircraft services had withdrawn the previous year, with the result that the only consistent flights in were regular airline services from Port Moresby. Another mission aviation operator was able to offer occasional limited assistance.

We were encouraged as we talked with the senior public servants and learnt more of their needs, to learn that many were Christians, something evident in their deep commitment to integrity, honesty and the welfare of their community.

In response to the growing requests from provincial leaders for services in their province, I started to look at other models of enterprise which would see more availability for provinces not currently serviced, but without extending us beyond what we could manage (which was very limited already).

As Christians we are called to make disciples, but the most effective way we can do that is by making disciple-makers. In other words, we make disciples who will in turn make more disciples. So in the same vein, what if we focused more on training others to develop and run their air operation rather than doing it all ourselves? What if we became facilitators for provinces to operate their own air service by providing the expertise in training and mentoring? Provincial governments had funding and resources available for rural services and the political will to provide such services for their people. We had the technical expertise, experience, a certified flight training school in-country, and a number of our pilots already held Instructor Pilot qualifications. We could actually increase air services capacity throughout the country this way, while meeting our own goals of spiritual transformation.

So my model considered an agreement with a provincial government in which they provided the infrastructure such as aircraft, airport facilities and accommodation, sponsored their own pilots for pilot training with us, and we allocated experienced pilots and other staff to work side by side with them to develop their operation.

This model was in embryo in my mind as we discussed possibilities with the Milne Bay leaders, who warmed to such a concept. One island group had already talked about buying their own aircraft as they contemplated mine royalties already in hand. It was a different approach to our traditional operation within PNG and as such would need more time to develop. By June I had a draft concept on paper, with a six year plan from signing the agreement to having a provincial operation fully functioning independently of MAF.

The plan we did start to discuss immediately was to send a Twin Otter from Goroka at least once a fortnight to Port Moresby, then out to the province, with availability to spend 24 hours flying in the area. Just as we did in the 1980s, this would provide opportunity for people to travel direct to their rural airstrip location from Port Moresby, as well as inter-port travel in the area, church travel and coffee exports from rural airstrips into Gurney, Alotau's main airport, included. We parted with a commitment to explore how we could facilitate this option.

I was optimistic that we were on the verge of being able to reach out to this community at least with some assistance. However, despite ongoing discussions during the year, both the ability to release a Twin Otter and manage the logistics to serve Milne Bay, and the development of the new model engaging provincial governments, were not able to progress. Pierre's accident a month later intervened.

Recruiting enough pilots and engineers to man the PNG program was always a challenge. At one point we were down to five pilots available for duties around the country! We had to continually review our staffing and where our resources were maintained. In the long run, it seemed to me that the best way forward for us was to be training others rather than trying to do it ourselves, which was the traditional MAF approach, especially in a time of shortage.

One of the hardest decisions for me was the Leadership Team decision to close down the Kawito supply base on the Aramia River in the Western Province. Established in the 1960's, its origins as a supply depot were at Wasua on the Fly River, which was moved to Kawito in the early 1970s. The channel by which coastal shipping vessels could sail into the jetty at Wasua began to silt up, eventually becoming indistinguishable from the grassy swampland around it.

The Aramia River, just north of the Fly River, was deep and wide enough for coastal vessels, so an airstrip was built at Kawito and the mission concerned (APCM) moved staff there to maintain it. When Kathy and I arrived there to take up the pilot role in 1977, there was a small hangar to house the aircraft, a C206; a larger distribution store fed by the coastal ships from Port Moresby; and a handful of mission houses, one occupied by an APCM family, another by the store manager, and one allocated to the MAF pilot family. And of course the airstrip, cut out of the surrounding bush. The river provided the only access in and out apart from the aircraft. No roads existed through this large swampland. On the other side of the airstrip a village like community had sprung up with housing for the local staff engaged to work in the store and mission, which maintained a workshop to enable manufacture and maintenance of equipment and machinery. The resident missionary couple, Rudi, an engineer, and Margaret, a nurse, had endeared themselves to the local people through their help in maintaining outboard motors and medical/health care.

During those pioneering years for MAF in the 1960s and into the 1970s, the work focused on supporting the growing number of pioneering missionaries who trekked into inhospitable terrain to contact and live among at times inhospitable people. Some were known cannibals or head-hunters. As they spent months and months cutting an airstrip out of the jungle, with their local helpers filling valleys and levelling hills, we supported them by air drops from the Cessna C185 aircraft used by MAF in those early days.

Air dropping was an art. I was very thankful to have some of MAF's most experienced field pilots mentor me in the process. The right-hand side door of the C185 aircraft would be taken off by removing its two hinge pins. The middle seats were removed and a long seat belt attached to the rear seat belt attachment points. The cargo handler, usually another pilot, would sit on the small back bench seat with coffee bag size, hessian bags loaded with goods in front of him. As they approached the drop site, the handler would move the bags near the open door, but was restricted from falling out of the aircraft by the restraining belt.

The height of the aircraft above the ground for the drop was critical. If it was too low, the cargo bag may bounce up and hit the aircraft's tail feathers. If too high, the bag risked being smashed to pieces from the impact. I recall one air drop I did while we were based at Telefomin, at what became the Frieda River mine-site base, where the drop zone was a half-sized basketball court surrounded by jungle and a couple of buildings. We managed to get two bags out the door before climbing out over the trees with full power and returning to drop two more. I heard later that the eggs that were inside one of the bags survived the drop!

We had manned Kawito base as our first MAF base from late 1977 to mid 1980 and knew the area and people well. Later on, a pilot family had also been stationed at Rumginae in the upper reaches of the Western Province. That aircraft expanded the reach of the MAF program by doubling flight capacity in the province. However, by mid 2005 we were facing such a shortage of pilots that some MAF programs in the country were without any pilot. Politics and the reality of needing to equitably share resources around the mission areas meant we had to review the luxury of having two bases in the Western Province. I should add, this was not a luxury in the real sense of the word, as withdrawing from Kawito would reduce the capacity to service the area by the Rumginae aircraft alone by 50%. The province would suffer.

The role of the MAF aircraft had changed since our time at Kawito some 25 years earlier. The missionaries were now well established in their communities, and medical aid posts and schools had grown up beside churches and trade stores. MAF was now servicing those communities, the majority still only accessible by air.

It was a difficult decision and I certainly felt that I had betrayed our friends in the community. But it was a decision that had to be made to give other areas access to at least one aircraft. The Vanimo base was identified as needing a pilot and so Chris and his family were asked to relocate there, at the north-western tip of PNG.

Vanimo was a completely different situation which led to a very quick and unfortunate abandonment of the base and housing, and much stress to Chris and his family.

The administrative headquarters for the West Sepik or Sandaun Province, Vanimo is situated on the north coast just a few miles from the border with Indonesian Papua. The Vanimo and Wewak crews had played a significant role in the Aitape tsunami relief efforts in July 1988, when a series of four metre high waves pulverised coastal villages on the north coast of PNG. Entire generations were among the 2,200 people reportedly wiped out following a 7.0 earthquake off the coast. A Twin Otter was based there with two missionary pilots and their families. But the retirement of one and relocation of another left the base vacant. So a GA8 was now based there with a one pilot operation until we could transfer in a second pilot.

Just a few months after transferring there, I received a worrying call from Chris at Vanimo advising that a vehicle load of men had come to their house and made threats, indicating they were about to take over the house - Chris and his family needed to get out. It was a very intimidating experience for the families as the men were brandishing machetes.

We immediately assessed the situation as being high risk and unacceptable for the family to continue. So they packed up quickly and flew the aircraft out, closing the base to resident operations. Once again we knew this would be to the distinct disadvantage of the people in the community who depended on our air transport, but we could not allow the family to be intimidated and threatened like this. There was obvious disappointment that the lease agreement, and the work and expense to maintain the houses, had been trashed so easily.

The problem had arisen as the houses our two staff used had been leased long term from the government Housing Corporation. They were ex-military accommodation, overlooking the ocean from the hill on a headland, good houses, which MAF maintained in excellent condition as part of the lease arrangements. Not long before, I had received a call from the Housing Corporation asking if we wanted to continue to use the houses. I advised the senior Housing Corporation person very clearly that we were happy to keep paying rent on both houses as we needed them for our own operational staff. Due to the shortage of pilots, we had reduced to one pilot while we prepared to locate a second pilot there. It did mean however that one of the houses was vacant for a couple of months.

This had come to the attention of a local leader and politician who now felt that it should be made available to local people, probably himself! It was his thugs who arrived to menace the pilot, apparently having been told by the Housing Corporation that the houses *were* available, a complete untruth! I was unsure if the untruth was from the Housing Commission or the politician! I did later have a discussion with the Housing Commission Chairman who offered an apology, but it was all over by then.

Chris and his family hastily packed up as best they could and relocated to Wewak next day.

It was difficult to try and explain the situation to the community. We sought to continue to operate flights in the province a couple of days a week using Wewak based aircraft but the service would be reduced. I was told that there were even voices in parliament asking why MAF was no longer serving the province, apparently suggesting we should be disciplined for our lack of service! Our response could only be that the matter was not what we envisaged, and the politician who precipitated it should be the one to answer any questions. Without adequate and safe housing for our staff families, we could not base pilots and aircraft there.

We have so much goodwill within the communities we serve in PNG and so it is challenging when we are confronted with opposition like this, especially from community leaders who seemed to have no idea of the ramifications for the wider community of their actions. I am thankful that occurrences like this are few and far between.

Kos and I returning from Killerton Island

Old water hole and overgrown wall ruins of the earliest missionary outreach into PNG on Killerton Island, Milne Bay Province.

21. NEW OPPORTUNITIES

As we moved into 2007, two events caused me to question if there were changes we could make to the PNG flight operation which would enhance our service to the airstrip communities.

One of these was that a small regional airline, Airlink, closed its doors. They operated Cessna 404's and were planning to introduce an ATR aircraft to their fleet. But then suddenly they collapsed. This left a hole in the market, and meant that a number of legs between rural towns no longer had air services. The only alternative was long drives on poorly maintained roads between towns such as Goroka and Madang. This left a gap that we could consider filling on several routes that we serviced mainly for our own internal positioning needs. In particular, the multi-leg route from Madang to Goroka, then to Mt Hagen and on to Wewak, was one we already flew sometimes. But our own requirement to be able to ferry staff, aircraft, paperwork or freight regularly, opened up a possible opportunity for us.

I presented the situation to the PNG Board at their meeting. It was an interesting concept, starting up a regular flight each Monday morning to fly Madang to Wewak and return, via Goroka and Mt Hagen. The PNG Board members had certainly noticed the departure of Airlink and showed keen support for the idea that MAF could service the community through these flights. After all, all that was changing was the addition of a fixed schedule; we were already flying those routes on a demand basis. Some of the Board members posed the question as to whether MAF would consider also expanding into the larger airliner type aircraft, such as a Dash 8. They saw it as a great way for MAF to become more broadly community focused in its services. The Board Chairman was reluctant to pursue the latter idea but recognised the positive Board feelings about my proposition.

It would mean making some changes, mainly training staff to be able to be more focused on getting the aircraft loaded and refuelled on each leg in time to meet the planned ETD. So we embarked on a training process to do this, something every other airline in the world does on a regular basis. But the discipline required would challenge our airport traffic staff, who were used to an 'on-demand' schedule, not a time-clock schedule! With our C206, recently introduced GA Airvan, and current Twin Otter fleet, we had flexibility to schedule which aircraft was appropriate on each leg based on booking demand.

The feedback from our PNG staff was generally positive but the response from our international missionary staff was very mixed. Some expressed very strongly that they did not see flying a commercial route as 'mission' flying. However, a large part of MAF's flying operations was genuine commercial operations, flying everything from trade store goods to missionary food and church, medical or educational supplies, as well as people from every walk of life. Government workers such as teachers and health workers had airfares paid for by the government. Missionaries paid a subsidised price because the rest of the operation provided the bulk of revenue needed to operate. So to me, and I believe the Board, the distinction between what we were already doing (mission flying) and conducting flights for the same people over the same routes but on a fixed schedule, was minuscule. It only added to the depth of the service we could add, not detract from it.

So we did staff training and then commenced the flight as proposed. It was able to return some revenue on these legs now whereas there may have otherwise been little or no revenue when run purely for MAF operational reasons, such as pilot movements or aircraft swaps. One of the things you try to avoid at all costs is to run an aircraft over a route without on average generating at least an income that covers operating costs. I hoped that we would now find these flights brought a financial advantage as well as a practical one.

The flights ran for several weeks, maybe a couple of months, before we withdrew the schedule. The main reason was that the variables involved to schedule the right aircraft, matching with bookings, and the commitment required by each airport base on the route to meet the on-time demands, proved too arduous. I was disappointed we couldn't make it happen, but one learns that pragmatism must sometimes be applied to dreams!

During this time a meeting was held between senior MAFI and the MAF Leadership team to consider fleet requirements for the future. The faithful C206 was being phased out and replaced by the GA8 Airvan. While the Airvan came with glowing expectations of being a STOL aircraft, it did not fully meet expectations, particularly as criteria used for "P" (Performance) charts which help determine airstrip performance were more stringent than previously anticipated. MAFI worldwide was operating the Cessna Caravan as its standard aircraft of choice now, and as MAF Australia was being absorbed into MAF International, there was expectation of fleet standardisation in PNG. One of the big issues is that we were operating to many short marginal airstrips. These were bread and butter work for the C206, and had been for many years. Our initial concerns that the Caravan may not have capability to operate to these more marginal community airstrips were reduced with the expectation of a "Hot Wings" Caravan wing modification, which reduced approach speeds to enable landing at shorter airstrips.

With AVGAS shortages being forecast, the Caravan operated with a Pratt & Whitney turbine engine similar to the Twin Otter's, using AVTUR (Jet fuel), fully available within PNG. So the scene was set to divest the piston engined, AVGAS burning C206 and GA8. While the Twin Otters were a marvellous workhorse, able to land on basically every airstrip, they were old and needed continuing expensive maintenance.

There were other single engine turbine aircraft appearing or already in the market. The Pilatus Porter was long established in its class and used by MAF US across the border in Indonesian Papua. Two newer types, the PAC750 and Kodiak Quest, were still relatively unproven, though another mission was preparing to use the Kodiak. We had been able to have a demonstration flight in the PAC750 on a tour to potential operators. However all three types were considered inferior to the Caravan by MAFI for various reasons.

So at the conclusion of the meeting it was clear that the Twin Otter would also be phased out and MAF PNG would become a single fleet type operator with Cessna Caravans. It would of course take several years for the phase out to happen. It also required a new regime of pilot training and engineering infrastructure to introduce the Caravan. Unfortunately the 'Hot Wings' company also folded, undermining some performance expectations. It was encouraging to see some evidence of pilot recruitment improving, with several pilots from the wider MAFI network joining the team.

22. FLIGHT CO-ORDINATION

The second event which promted me to consider changes we could make to the PNG flight operation was a Twin Otter flight from Telefomin to Mt Hagen I was a passenger on, with the aircraft flying in basically empty for scheduled maintenance. On the same morning, another Twin Otter flew from Mt Hagen to Vanimo to take a load of passengers to Telefomin, and then flew on to Mt Hagen empty. Two aircraft flew four legs of 1 hour or more with only one leg for one of the aircraft carrying a payload (and earning revenue). It made no operational sense to me.

So the vision was born of a way to ensure there was connection between each of the MAF bases around the country (see the map on page xiv) to avoid duplication of flights across provincial borders. My concept was based around what we called Community Service Flights (CSF).

This was the idea: each base would run a basic schedule of flights around the airstrip communities in its area of operation (often a province) for 2 to 4 days a week. Some research would be applied, usually based on the pilots' local knowledge of their airstrips, so that those airstrips with higher demand would receive more flights. Then each base would have availability to add in ad hoc flights as needed. This would ensure that every airstrip community received a flight for mail, medevacs and basic services at least once a month. At the same time, any flights which extended beyond the borders of its provincial responsibility would be communicated to a central programming co-ordinator in Mt Hagen. The Coordinator's responsibility was to ensure that duplication was minimised, which in turn should see more efficient use of the aircraft. It also helped maximise payload opportunities for aircraft travelling in and out of Mt Hagen for scheduled maintenance, particularly 100 hourly checks.

Once again there was a mixed response from the international staff. Some saw it as a great idea and ran with it, in fact making it a very successful way of operating in their base. But others did not see it as of such value and so did not really support it. As time went by, I realised that the success of the initiative lay very squarely in the willingness of the pilots at each base to make it work.

One of the key people required was a central Coordinator. We needed someone who was a very lateral thinker, could juggle a number of balls (or aircraft!) in the air at once, understood the complex MAF PNG operation well, and who could find solutions quickly. We found that person in one of the pilot's wives, Jenny, a former lawyer who had excelled in programming the aircraft at a couple of bases already, and in building significant relationship with our travelling customers. This position did become a key one for the PNG program into the future, and, as does any such position, was adapted and moulded around the personality and skills of the person in the job, and the flexibility of the changing needs of the flight operation.

While I believe the CSF concept did start to work well in a couple of single pilot bases, and continued on in principle under future General Managers, overall it did not gain the traction to become a significant modus operandi in the other bases, particularly the multi-pilot bases, where demand shouted louder than isolation.

23. ELECTION TIME STRATEGIES

Election year, 2007. The Leadership Team started planning months in advance. PNG is no stranger to election related violence as dominant political personalities seeking allegiance fuel inter-clan tensions. Previous elections made it clear that the carriage of ballot boxes and campaigning politicians were both high risk scenarios. Shots had been fired at aircraft carrying ballot boxes. So the Leadership Team made a decision that we would only carry empty ballot boxes and would not carry candidates who were campaigning. I wrote to the Electoral Commissioner advising this. However, we were approached by the Police and Defence Force to transport their personnel to polling stations in several places, which we did.

During the previous elections there had been violence in a number of places including Mt Hagen. MAF staff in the town had witnessed extreme acts of violence, including destruction of property and assault. The feeling was that it could be worse this time and therefore contingency plans were drawn up and put into place. Many hours were spent in meetings and prayer during the months leading up to the elections. The LT decision was that most staff would move out of Mt Hagen and relocate for several weeks to coastal locations such as Madang and Wewak, and other safe highlands locations such as Telefomin. A skeleton contingency of local staff was left in Mt Hagen. As expected, some international staff did not agree with the decision, feeling it was not supporting our local staff.

Kathy and I elected to move to Telefomin, partly because it was familiar territory and partly because it now had a satellite phone and good radio communications with the rest of the bases. A little earlier an Australian couple who were video producers had been in contact, offering to record a good news story on MAF at no cost. They were also doing a story on the elections, particularly in the Sepik area. I invited them to come and spend a week with us at Telefomin and film what they wanted. It was an unscripted effort, shooting footage with the aim of making a story out of it. They had lots of opportunity to film election happenings, including security forces coming and going on MAF flights. As it happened in real life, the weather turned bad and we had a situation where our aircraft could not get airborne and fly in the aircraft fuel we required, or top up the trade stores with enough food to support the community. Then there was drama with a Twin Otter nose wheel going flat, and bird nests found in an exhaust pipe. Finally the rain ceased and we were able to redeem the situation. It all made for a good story. I discovered that I was featured in it in a number of scenes and that my voice was actually considered good for much of the narration.

When the production, a 55 minute video titled *"Above and Beyond"* was finished,[6] MAF decided to screen it in a theatre in Melbourne, advising supporters. I was able to attend in conjunction with other MAF business in Australia at that time. I think it is one of the best MAF promotional videos ever precisely because it was not made as a promotional – it just tells the story as it happened. Unfortunately I am not sure if its potential was really explored by MAF beyond the cinema screening. The creators did submit it into a Pacific area media competition and I believe it was screened on an Australian national TV channel at one stage. For me, my sole CD copy is an excellent reminder of our life and work in PNG with

---
6. For online link to the video, see page 169.

MAF at that time, something historically that my children and grandchildren can take into the future.

The election period overall went without major incident around the towns, for which we were thankful. We were amused to discover that due to ammunition shortages, many of the armed soldiers who provided oversight at election booths did not actually have any real ammunition. The requirement for ammunition to be stored separately on flights alerted us to that! Despite the security, at Telefomin we were told that a bundle of rigged voting papers was found in one ballot box, apparently deposited there clandestinely by one of the scrutineers!

Filming the documentary from inside a Twin Otter.

Morning fog at Telefomin.

Election posters at a local trade store, Telefomin.

Grasslands and village houses in the Telefomin valley,
Sepik Gorge in the background.
(from original watercolour)

24. ADVISING GOVERNMENT

In September 2007, I met with the Minister for Transport and Civil Aviation, Hon. Don Polye MP, who called in to our Mt Hagen offices. He invited us to submit a paper which could provide data and ideas to the government to benefit the rural aviation sector, and ultimately, rural communities. With the help of our administrative team, I drafted a paper titled *'The Challenge of a Viable and Sustainable Rural Aviation Industry in PNG'*, which was submitted to the Minister in October 2007.

There were several key issues which we had already been discussing for some time, so this opportunity to present these directly to government was a gift to us. The key issues we raised were:

- The negative economic climate for rural aviation operators - aviation was being driven by a mining and exploration boom which was throwing big bucks into these operations, but services to local communities were struggling. Some operators were actively cutting back their air services to rural airstrips to meet their contractual mining obligations.
- The shortage of pilots and engineers, both a local and global issue.
- Spiralling operating costs caused by rapidly increasing fees from government aviation agencies (such as

enroute, landing and airport charges) as well as fuel and insurance costs.

- The resultant subsequent reduction in service capacity by (mainly christian mission) operators to rural areas.

We proposed seven strategies to the government to reduce operational costs for rural operators and increase their service capability.

1. Aviation Fuel Costs

In 2004 a new Interoil refinery at Napa Napa near Port Moresby commenced refining PNG oil, including production of JetA1 aviation fuel, used by turbine and jet engined aircraft.[7] We expected that this would reduce the cost of buying imported fuel. However, it appears the contract allowed the refinery to sell aviation fuel locally at *international/imported* prices. We found it hard to understand why the government would allow this - and not allow the country to benefit from the production of its own oil products. The price of JetA1 rose by 58% in the 12 months to January 2005, and 77% to September 2007.

To put this into perspective for MAF operations, we calculated that the fuel cost for operating a Twin Otter aircraft was about K21,000 (about AU$10,000) more in September 2007 than in January 2004. MAF PNG now operated three Twin Otters. We calculated that we had absorbed more than K2 million (AU$1m) in increased fuel costs alone in the first two years of the Napa Napa operation.

With the advent of single engine turbine aircraft such as the Cessna Caravan and PAC 750, operators were obviously keen to introduce these types and half their fuel costs.

However civil aviation regulations were not keeping up

---

7. AVGAS used for piston engined aircraft had to be imported still, incurring import duty. MAF PNG operated 10 piston engined aircraft, Cessna 206 & GA8 Airvans.

with the rapid growth of innovation and technology within the aviation industry. This was particularly the case with the introduction of satellite-based GPS technology. While the government was committed in principle to sole use GPS/GNS navigation, the regulations still required a land based alternative for landing approaches. This was not made any easier by the few current land based aids, ADFs and VORs, which were difficult to maintain and becoming obsolete and so often unserviceable. This issue came hand in hand with the regulations which prohibited IFR[8] commercial passenger operations in single engined aircraft. So both the prohibition on single engined IFR operations for passengers and the inability to use sole GPS technology effectively meant operators could not move ahead to maximise the benefits of single engine turbine aircraft, and the resultant cost benefit from operating one engine against two.

So our recommendation to the government was to investigate the huge rise in JetA1 costs and see if *"other interests may be profiting unnecessarily"*. We also noted that economic sustainability in this area must be supported by *"CAA adopting a positive approach to the introduction of single engine turbine aircraft including through legislation..."*[9]

2. Rural Aviation Fuel Subsidy

This idea had been raised earlier by the government itself, and we wholeheartedly supported it.

MAF maintained fuel stocks at twelve locations around PNG. Drum stock fuel was transported to these locations by coastal vessel from Port Moresby or Lae (eg. Madang,

---
8. Flight by instruments only, ie. in cloud and allowing landing in poor weather when conditions were below minimum visual (VFR) standards for visibility and cloud.
9. While PNG Air Services continued to publish GPS Instrument Approaches and expand GNS resources for operators, it would be 15 years before IFR flight for passengers in single engine turbine aircraft (Caravans) would be approved by PNG CAA.

Wewak, Vanimo, Kawito, Kiunga), trucks (eg. from Lae up the Highlands Highway to Goroka, Mt Hagen, Mendi and Tari), and by aircraft to isolated locations such as Telefomin. In 2006 the cost of sea and road freight added K.26t (AU$.13c) per litre to the fuel cost (10% extra). However the cost of airfreighting fuel added an additional K2.16 (AU$1.08) per litre. These transportation costs added nearly K400,000 (AU$200,000) to our 2006 operational costs. So we recommended establishing this fund to subsidise rural operators for the additional transportation costs for fuel to service rural communities.

3. Tax Incentives

While an earlier approach was knocked back as impossible under existing legislation, we knew that there were tax credit schemes legislated for mining companies and requested the government to consider appropriate tax reduction initiatives for rural aviation operators.[10]

4. CSO value to offset some operational costs

This strategy requested that Treasury cover the cost of all CAA and other specific government operational charges directly, based on the value of flights which are recognised as fulfilling the government's 'Community Service Obligation' (CSO) to rural communities.[11]

Every MAF flight record contains a breakdown of loading to provide a clear and comprehensive record of who and what travelled. In 2006 the value of medevac, health and education travel, plus community development, particularly produce brought in from rural areas (mostly coffee), was K2.2m (AU$1.1m). MAF was paying about K200,000 per year

---

10. I am not aware of any subsequent government initiatives to 2 and 3. However MAF Management and Board continued to make submissions to the government in all these areas with a number of positive responses over the years.

11. The PNG Civil Aviation Act 2000 states: "6. Matters of National Importance. A person exercising a power or function under this Act shall recognise and provide for the following of national importance... (d) the maintenance of air services to provincial and rural communities."

for CAA charges such as surveillance, landing and airport charges, but these were increased in 2007, by up to 62% for surveillance charges and 20% for landing charges. We proposed that this represented only 10% of the value of CSO services genuinely flown by MAF and so could be genuinely offset by the government.

This proposal did receive the government's positive attention and legislation was passed in the next couple of years which approved Treasury paying both PNG Air Services Ltd (en route, navigation and surveillance) and National Airports Corporation - NAC (airport and landing) charges directly on behalf of charges incurred by rural operators. PNGASL embraced this and has continued to not charge rural operators, including MAF, though has met costs from its own revenue[12] as the mechanism to activate Treasury payments was not finalised. NAC did not follow through with this immediately but, in time, significant concessions to rural operators have been introduced.

5. Funding to Improve Rural Airstrip Standards

Many of the more than 500 airstrips that MAF in PNG operates to were built decades earlier. With little maintenance over the years, a number were in such poor shape now that about a quarter of the airstrips on our books were closed because of significant maintenance issues. This equated to well over 100 communities now isolated as very few have alternative modes of transportation in and out. Many others were still open but causing excessive wear and tear on the aircraft, and liable to be closed temporarily due to rain or long grass. The cost of a propeller strike, undercarriage damage or underbelly pod damage is high, and further damage requiring an engine replacement, for example, can cost hundreds of thousands of dollars.

---
12. PNG Air Services budgeted about Kina 500,000 a year for this.

So we saw a great need to seek to catalyse a service which would be able to tackle this issue of maintenance at rural airstrips, and so provide services to those communities otherwise isolated.

This proposal did find acceptance but it would take another seven years.[13] The Rural Airstrip Agency (RAA) has, since 2014, significantly improved the condition of dozens of rural airstrips, and met our initial hopes for a government funded, dedicated agency to do so.

6. Direct Grants

From time to time various grants become available for specific purposes, such as to meet needs at specific times such as drought or floods, to subsidise the air freight costs of coffee from remote communities, for specialised flights in a province, or other specific needs.[14]

7. Increasing pilot numbers

This is one area where we could already contribute through our flying school in Mt Hagen. The biggest challenge for PNG pilot trainees was finding sponsorship to pay for the cost of gaining a Commercial Pilot Licence (over K100,000). We encouraged the government to initiate scholarship funding.

---

13. In 2013, the Minister for Civil Aviation, Hon Davis Stephen MP, initiated a 'Civil Aviation and Rural Airstrips and Air Services Forum' in Mt Hagen, attended by over 100 representatives from industry. This led to the Minister initiating the formation of a public partnership agency called the Rural Airstrip Agency (RAA), and the allocation of K6m of government funds. From small beginnings RAA has continued to grow and provide airstrip upgrading and restoration as well as training for local airstrip maintenance workers, supplying mowers and expertise. MAF has continued to work very closely with RAA..

14. Over the next few years MAF did receive grants at both a provincial level and national level, such as that by the Coffee Industry Corporation (CIC) which subsidised the air freight costs for coffee farmers in remote areas, and in 2011 the government of PNG (Hon Don Polye was Finance Minister) allocated MAF PNG a grant of K1m towards offsetting travel subsidies and associated capital costs.

25. ORO FLOOD EMERGENCY

PNG is known for its rain. Yes, but there are also dry seasons and times when the rain holds back. During our time at Kawito in the late 1970's, we experienced a drought in the Western Province. People knew that this came in a seven year cycle back then. There was no rain for several months and we had been recycling water for some time. Washing water became laundry water which was then used for the toilet. The Aramia River dropped to record lows and surrounding swamplands became dry ground. As water tanks began to reach their last rungs, it became a matter for prayer in the church and community. I recall that our tank was at the last low rung when the rains came in again. A missionary family at Suki, near the border with Indonesian West Papua, had a cattle project but had run out of drinking water. So I flew out containers of water for them, and in return, they filled a container with fresh milk for us!

When it does rain though, it buckets down. The terrain is used to it and so generally the waters run off, quickly finding their way into the many small streams leading into the major river systems such as the Waghi, Strickland, Fly and Sepik Rivers. From time to time though there is an exceptional weather system which sends extraordinary rains which cause flooding and devastation. This was the situation in the Oro Province, when late in November 2007 I received reports of flooding causing gardens and even villages to be swept away.

My first flying job in 1974, flying a C206, was a posting to Popondetta township, the capital of the Oro Province, on the north side of the island northeast across the ranges from Port Moresby. Macair employed me as a fresh 210 hour Commercial pilot. I had previously worked with them in 1972-73 as a Traffic Officer, so was familiar with their operations at ground level. It was a single pilot, one aircraft operation based out of Girua airport, one of several runways in the area constructed during WWII. I spent the year flying to all the small airstrips in the area, carrying people and goods in and out, and agricultural produce such as cardamom and chilli often back into Girua. So from an aviation operational perspective, I knew this area very well.

Popondetta also held an attraction because of a missionary family I was getting to know who were doing Bible translation in the coastal language (Notu/Ewage) which encompassed the Oro Bay villages as well as Buna and Gona. This coastline was the focus of the WWII Japanese invasion forces with their quest to cross the Owen Stanley Ranges to conquer Port Moresby, via what became known as the Kokoda Trail. I would often spend weekends staying with the family at their Beama (Oro Bay) village house, about 30km drive from Popondetta township. I unashamedly had ulterior motives – their daughter Kathy and I had commenced a friendship. While she was not there for much of the time, having completed high school and active in missionary support work elsewhere in PNG, it was valuable time building relationships with her parents and younger siblings. It paid off when Kathy and I were engaged at the end of that year!

In the 1960s MAF had based an aircraft out of Popondetta to serve the Anglican church, which was the dominant church in the area. However MAF had had no permanent presence there since then, only occasional flights by the Port Moresby based aircraft.

I was sure that there was an immediate need in the province that we could respond to. Reports of food gardens being covered in mud up to a metre deep came through. There had been a number of deaths in flood waters. The most disturbing was to hear that the village of Beama, my parents-in-law's former village, had been washed into the sea, with some people also swept out as well. It was clear that this was an environmental and humanitarian disaster of unheard-of proportions for PNG. The government called in the Australian Defence Force to assist and so a contingent of fixed wing and rotary wing aircraft were soon gathered at Girua airport.

I quickly proposed a plan to send a Twin Otter down to Girua as soon as possible to assist where it could, though we had little idea how that might be. Reports were that most of the bush airstrips had suffered damage. The ADF helicopters began carrying out inspections of the airstrips so that their serviceability could be known prior to any fixed wing aircraft landings. We also recognised that food shortages would be a problem for many of the communities. So I approached the Anglican Bishop in Mt Hagen, where there is a strong Anglican presence as well, with the idea of filling up the Twin Otter with local donated produce to take down to Girua. Two days later our Goroka based Twin Otter, flown by two experienced pilots, Richard and Greg, loaded up with about a tonne of fresh produce, mainly root vegetables such as sweet potato, and flew down to Girua.

MAF Australia assigned a former MAF pilot, Tom, to come up and liaise with the ADF and government officials in Popondetta and coordinate our efforts. We were both able to join in various meetings with other response stakeholders as part of the larger efforts. The aircraft returned to the highlands the following weekend, and loaded up again with vegetables before spending a second week out of Girua. As the ADF cleared airstrips as suitable for fixed wing operations, we were able to then fly in to them and provide assistance and bring relief. It was a very satisfying initiative in response to a very pressing emergency, one we were glad to assist in.

Normally we work on the basis of payment for flights, either through ticket sales, freight per kilo, or charter quote at the time of the flight. But I stepped out in faith here and offered our services at no cost. We could worry about costs later. I was pleased to subsequently hear that our efforts on the ground were very well received and in fact fundraising efforts in Australia and beyond had supported this emergency project very well.

Flooded rivers in the Oro Province.

Unloading flood relief food from the highlands at Itokama (above) and Tufi (below).

26. GUNSHOTS

While we learnt to "expect the unexpected" in PNG, there were times when we could not have even expected the unbelievable!

For some months one Wewak ground staffer had been carefully attending to a plant growing in front of the terminal as a pretty bush. But when an alert pilot noticed the plant as he was taxiing out one day, it led to some red faces. The worker had not realised that he was cultivating a marijuana plant!

In Mt Hagen, an MAF mini-bus collecting staff for work one morning was hijacked. Everyone on board was ordered out of the vehicle and it was driven off by the thieves, who wore balaclavas and toted guns. Shots were fired in the air. When we contacted the Police they advised that they could not assist because they had run out of fuel in their vehicles! We put an aircraft up to see if it could see the bus from the air but to no avail.

After advertising a reward, a day or two later three local men made contact to advise they had been able to retrieve the mini-bus from the thieves and were ready to get the reward. I advised that we were happy to give the reward if the vehicle was returned with no damage, information leading to the identification of the thieves provided, and the reward would be handed over in public with community leaders present. Next day the men sought to bargain for a higher reward, but no raise in the reward was offered. A day or two later the vehicle was discovered having been trashed. From then on we painted "MAF" in large black letters on the roof of all our vehicles.

A much more rewarding surprise encounter came when two casually dressed men came to see me at the hangar in Mt Hagen, introducing themselves as David Meyer (Joyce Meyer's son) and Mark Zschech (Hillsong singer Darlene Zschech's husband). They were networking, representing their respective ministries, in preparation for a visit by Joyce Meyer in the next year or so. We spent some time talking about opportunities and networks in the local churches. Feeling that I should honour their visit by taking them to lunch at a nearby airport hotel restaurant, I quickly ducked into Accounts and persuaded the accounts staff to give me some cash to cover the meal cost, equivalent to less than US$100.

The meal was slow in coming but the half chicken, standard serving in PNG, was enjoyed by all, and continued our opportunity to discuss their upcoming ministry venture. Once back at the office and preparing to depart, David Meyer said he would like to make a small donation, and would be expected to do so by their ministry. He casually placed US$1,000 in my hand. I was, of course, very appreciative of his generosity, and couldn't help joking to the accounts staff that this was a pretty good return on what they had invested in me an hour or two earlier!

Joyce Meyer did visit and MAF was very involved as part of the network of churches and ministries participating in her outreach, which included Australian country gospel singer, Steve Grace, but I had already completed my time as GM and was out of PNG by the time this happened.

MAFI engaged the services of a professional psychologist to provide support for staff on the field. Based in Toowoomba, west of Brisbane, he was also a private pilot with an interest in aviation. In 2007 arrangements were made for he and his wife to visit PNG to gain some insight into life on the field.

Kathy and I hosted them at our house in Mt Hagen for a few days. On Saturday afternoon we took them to dinner at a local resort-hotel, The Highlander, one of only a few places where we could eat out. As we drove from our house to the hotel, we passed an open area near the shopping centre and saw a crowd of people start running across the field. Suddenly a police car came tearing round the corner in front of us and stopped beside the road. In a matter of seconds, as we approached the police car, some policemen jumped out of it, brandishing weapons. They started shooting at the crowd, presumably rubber bullets or blanks, just as we drove up beside them! Then, a little further along, as we turned a corner, we saw a mass of people, some holding rocks, blocking the road ahead. Fortunately the next turn off to the hotel was just in front of the crowd, and I quickly turned in there. 200 metres later we were safe in the hotel car park.

It was a very traumatic and frightening experience for our new friends to PNG. We quickly assessed the scenario and realised there was no need to be overly concerned. This was the aftermath of a Saturday football match, with supporters from both sides expressing their passion... perhaps some with a desire to equalise the score! We assured our friends that this was not an everyday event, but you have to be ready all the time for something unexpected to happen here. As the tourism posters state, in PNG 'expect the unexpected'. I'm sure it gave our psychologist friend some valuable personal experience into life here!

I was also able to seek for some review of my own situation and a little later received a letter from him with his formal diagnosis. I was in burnout with possible PTSD.

27. CAA CONTACT

One of our new pilots, Matt, found that his flight bag had gone missing as he came through Port Moresby enroute to Mt Hagen. He had placed his bag onto the security screening conveyor while he went through the security doorway, but when he came to pick up his bag on the other side, it was missing. A search had yielded nothing. This was no small thing as it contained all of his flight gear as well as personal items and money. It was ludicrous to think that it had gone missing in the two metre distance from one side of the screening machine to the other, but that is what happened.

I contacted the Civil Aviation Authority (CAA), who managed airport security at the time, and spoke with the Deputy CEO, an Australian working on contract in PNG. Subsequently I ended up visiting him during a trip to Port Moresby. He was very concerned about what had happened and approved 3,000 kina as compensation for the pilot. The compensation was never actually received, however it was the continuation of a valuable relationship with CAA management, building on the numerous contacts with them over the last three years. The flight bag turned up years later in Alotau airport terminal!

During 2007 I was invited by the government to join the CAA PNG Board and asked to attend meetings in early December. As Kathy and I would be going through Port Moresby enroute to attend our daughter's wedding in Sydney, the logistics seemed to fall into place.

28. COMPENSATION THREATS

One of the passengers in Pierre's aircraft was dragged out of the aircraft through a side window by over-zealous villagers who had rushed to the accident scene. At Kudjip hospital he was checked and assessed carefully. He was functionally a paraplegic however the doctor advised me that there was no sign of obvious nerve damage to his spine evident from their tests. We are not sure what caused the paraplegia but it appears most likely that it was a result of being dragged out of the aircraft by the over-zealous onlookers.

His family took up his cause and a brother began to visit me from time to time. He was particularly assertive in his dialogue with me, as some highlanders can be, raising the expectation that a sizable compensation of several million kina was expected by the family. Occasionally, as I walked home from the shops or market in Mt Hagen town, he would come alongside and walk with me, once again pleading his brother's case. I suspected it may have also reinforced the message that, 'we know where you live', but that did not bother me. I have never felt unsafe in PNG, nor been naive.

I felt sympathy for them. The passenger was confined to a wheelchair, something that is unmanageable in their mountainous village context. Other medical issues and needs he may be experiencing would also go unmet in the village.

We had handed the matter over to the insurance company but I made the mistake of being a touch point for them and the family, as the insurance company had no representative in Mt Hagen. It was a mistake. In the minds of the family, MAF was responsible for the accident and therefore compensation was our problem. My explanation that the insurance company would deal with it fell on deaf ears. I realised in retrospect that we needed to have a clear separation between the insurance company and MAF.

Part of the issue was that by PNG law, applicable compensation was capped at mere thousands. The family was not interested in such a small amount and therefore expected that MAF itself would need to pay the millions demanded. For us to do so would, of course, be illegal. Prior to one encounter with him I had printed a copy of the PNG law which stated the capped compensation. As he argued once again, I put down the paper on the table beside him and said to him, with matched passion, "This is the law. It is PNG law. It is your law. I cannot change it." I saw a faint smile at the corner of his mouth, perhaps acknowledgement that he would get no further today.

About a year and a half after the accident, well into 2007, I received a report that the family back in their airstrip community was going to take some sort of retaliation against MAF, perhaps damage an aircraft or worse, assault a pilot. We now needed the wisdom of Solomon to seek a resolution to this in a way which would honour the family but remove the risk to our pilots and aircraft. The highlands airstrip from which this family came was in the middle of a dominant language group with several airstrips in the area. Our immediate response was to cease all flying operations into the airstrips in the area.

I contacted the local Police Commander and the OIC of Airport Security in Port Moresby. We arranged a meeting in Mt Hagen of representatives from all the airstrips in that language group, which they would oversee. My intention was to see if this would make the brother and his family accountable to the rest of their language community. We scheduled a Twin Otter to go out to these airstrips and prearranged with them to have a representative ready to come into Mt Hagen. When the flight returned to Mt Hagen, the pilot reported there had been a scuffle between the brother and family members, who did not want him to get on the aircraft. However, he had come.

Once in the meeting, on the 11th September, 2007, I sat at the back as an observer as the Police Commander and OIC Airport Security took over, their expertise and authority obvious. The room in a local hotel was arranged in a horseshoe table layout which allowed all twenty or so of the men to see and hear each other face to face. Each person was asked for their opinion on the action the family may have proposed against MAF. One by one the representatives all expressed their very strong support for MAF and the negative consequences for them of our service not being available. Finally, the leaders confronted the brother, who reticently agreed that no action against MAF would be taken.

I say reticently because he knew that his family would not want to agree to this, and he must face them on his return. Early in December he came to see me again in my office. My secretary advised me he was waiting to see me, but I was not ready to have another argument with him. If I am honest, I have to say that frustration and an opportunity to finalise this issue drove me more than grace. But as he entered my office, I was shocked.

He held his heavily bandaged left hand up, but only two fingers protruded from the top.

"What happened to you?" I asked in genuine compassion for him.

He recounted the story. When he arrived back in the village, another brother was angry with him for coming to the meeting and raised a machete to kill him. The blade came down on his outstretched hand, raised to protect himself. It sliced down between his fingers, cutting two of them off, and continued right down into his wrist. He had it attended to at basic health services facilities but to me it looked a long way from being healed. Then I noticed his right hand. It was atrophied and therefore of limited functioning. He was humbled by the experience and I genuinely felt for him, with his own family now turning on him. Once again I had to reiterate that MAF was not in a position to offer additional compensation for the death of his brother. He left despondent but no longer angry.

His brother, the one who had been injured in the accident, passed away as a result of his injuries more than a year after the accident.

At Telefomin airport with the Eliptamin 'gap' at left, the lowest entry point to the valley from the east.

29. BREAKDOWN

Earlier in 2007, during a debrief with Alan and Meg following their confidential counselling visit with field staff, they offered some insights into how staff were feeling. We estimated that at the time of Pierre's accident, about half of our international staff team were new arrivals since the time of the MFQ accident thirteen months earlier. Bearing in mind that more international staff had arrived since the second accident, a growing number of staff were not so affected by the impact of the accidents. However the longer term ones were wearing down. Having the election contingency plan in place was helping but there were still uncertainties.

With a growing number of staff coming from countries other than the traditional recruiting grounds of Australia and New Zealand, there was a definite tension from cross-cultural misunderstandings within the international staff community. Not only was this apparent from contrasts between the emerging European MAF International corporate culture and traditional MAF Aus/NZ culture, but also between the people from these cultures themselves. Most seemed to be a reflection that Australians did things differently than Europeans.

With two decades of missionary service behind us, we had seen many missionaries come and go. Too many hit the ground running, ready to see their good ideas about what they judged was needed implemented. Too many had left little of value when they departed a few years later. Our conclusion, supported by missiological theory, was that missionary ministry is much more effective when we have taken the time to listen to the people and learn from them. So in my early briefs with new missionary arrivals I encouraged them to take the time to listen and learn, and by the end of their first year then decide where they want to channel their energies in local missionary service opportunities. Unfortunately this encouragement had been taken negatively by some, who thought I was stiffling them, rather than seeking to make them more effective as missionaries.

While it was frustrating to hear that some felt that I was being too autocratic, not delegating, and not listening to them, I appreciated Alan and Meg's honesty. I suspect that some of this related to how people from different cultures expected the manager to act. With all that had happened in the last two plus years, with all the hours spent in Leadership Team and other meetings with groups and individuals, with all that I had sought to do in recruitment and communication, and in all the issues that a field leader has to deal with which general rank and file are not participants in, I heard what Alan and Meg were saying, but felt there was little I could do myself to make drastic changes.

They did say though that people were concerned that we were wearing out and so I took comfort in that honest recognition. That gave support to my own communication with MAF HQ leadership of how I was struggling.

As we came into December 2007, Kathy went down to Sydney a week earlier than me to help in our daughter's wedding preparations. But on the Monday morning I came to work and suffered a breakdown. Three things that normally would be easy to deal with arose, and I could no longer handle them. One was that the brother of the accident victim turned up again to see me. The other two were internal issues with MAF staff. I felt I was in a system that was not working and among a people I could no longer understand.

Realising I had crossed a line with my capacity to cope, I called the MAFI leadership and advised that I would be travelling back to Australia as planned, via Port Moresby for the CAA Board meeting, but that I was not in a mental state to return. Advice from the psychologist was to take a minimum three months off, with a return to limited duties only for a period, which I knew would be impossible to manage in this environment. I would be packing up over the next week before heading off. While MAFI leadership had earlier respectfully agreed to transition me out of the role by mid 2008, I had reached my limit six months early.

I spent a couple of days in Port Moresby waiting for the CAA meeting to happen but in the end was advised that I would not be joining the CAA Board after all. It was a frustrating time as I felt I had wasted my time hanging around when I wanted to be heading home. As it was, I had booked on the last flight out of Port Moresby before my daughter's wedding, but could not bring it forward as all flights were full for the Christmas period.

Checking in finally for the flight back to Australia, I thought I was at the end of my tether. But there was one more surprise.

"We don't have any record of your booking," said the airline check-in officer.

I was beside myself emotionally, as now the probability of missing my daughter's wedding was almost 100%. Trying to keep calm, for the first and last time using my position as leverage, I replied, "I am the General Manager of MAF and I need to be on that flight for my daughter's wedding, can you see if there is any way I can make it, thank you."

The officer asked me to wait and to my absolute relief, came back to advise that they had found a seat for me. I look back and thank God for that intervention, but I was beyond thankfulness at the time, just appreciative that the rope that was dangling me over churning waters had swung me back over dry land. As I boarded at the last minute and the door closed behind me, I felt a surge of relief. Even that was short lived too as a bout of dysentery kept me busy during the flight, no doubt proof of the stress I was feeling!

As I flew down the next leg from Cairns to Sydney, I struck up conversation with the passenger next to me. He was a pastor, also flying out due to burnout!

The formal diagnosis of burnout and possible PTSD helped me label my feelings and was one of the most helpful aspects for me at that time. Knowing I was struggling without being able to know why had been difficult. With a diagnosis I could now move forward with a plan to recover, with continued support and advice from the Psychologist and my family. MAF graciously placed me on extended leave before completing this term of service.

One word of encouragement at that time came from an MAFI senior manager, who told me that he didn't know of anyone else who could have managed MAF PNG through this difficult period. It was in fact another confirmation that I was meant 'for a time like this', whether I felt like it or not. For that I am thankful to God, whose power is made strong in our weakness.

EPILOGUE

What a privilege it was to walk my daughter down the aisle two days later, so thankful to have made it to Sydney.

While I was not appointed to the CAAPNG Board, there was a valid reason. New Civil Aviation legislation had created four separate entities, being CAAPNG, PNG Air Services Limited (PNGASL), National Airports Corporation (NAC) and the Accident Investigation Commission (AIC). In 2008 I was appointed by the Minister for Civil Aviation as a founding Director and Deputy Chairman to the Board of PNG Air Services Ltd (later renamed NiuSky Pacific Ltd) representing the aviation sector, retiring in 2021. In 2012 I was also appointed for a three-year term as a Director of NAC. It was a privilege to be able to serve the government and people of PNG in these roles also.

After leaving PNG as General Manager, I was also invited to join the MAF PNG Board, a great privilege after working with them over the previous three years. This enabled me to maintain contact with the PNG operation but in a different capacity, until 2012.

After six months leave, I trained as a Flight Instructor which led to establishing an independent flight training school and charter operation at Coffs Harbour, NSW. I was able to assist with relief instructing at the Mt Hagen flight school a couple of times while the main instructor was on leave.

Kathy and I returned to MAF PNG in 2012 with roles in operational and safety management, training, and back into flying, completing our final tour of service in MAF in late 2015.

Mike & Kathy Jelliffe at the factory handover of the 100th GA8 Airvan to MAF.

POSTSCRIPT

The issue of mental health is a difficult one for missionaries and perhaps many Christians in general. While the bravado of the Aussie bushmen's stoic 'she'll be right' of past eras may still permeate some thinking, there has been a shift in coming to grips with the facts of mental health in modern missions. Should Christians, especially those involved in ministry, be exempt from burnout?

Christ's sufficiency is not in opposition to recognition of the intricacy of the human experience, body, mind and soul, or the need to recognise the safety valves God has created us with. When we find ourselves in stressful situations, whether physical or emotional, our challenge is not to deny but to discover God at work in the midst of the situation.

The Apostle Paul describes his own experience of this in 2 Corinthians 4:7-9 (NIV) - *"But we have this treasure in jars of clay to show that this all-surpassing power is from God and not from us. We are hard pressed on every side but not crushed; perplexed but not in despair; persecuted but not abandoned; struck down but not destroyed. We always carry around in our body the death of Jesus, so that the life of Jesus may also be revealed in our body."*

When an organisation does not have enough capacity to reasonably share the workload, the resultant overload can be devastating, especially when circumstances become chaotic or extreme. Our Christian work ethic so often means we feel obligated to keep going, especially when we feel no other option is available. So many missionaries and church workers have been in this situation.

I hope my story encourages others who find themselves in similar stressful situations to consider recognising that burnout and its associated symptoms are in fact markers telling us to make a change. There is a time to slow down, take a break, sometimes to get out of there. Our body, created by God, is giving us directions, whether that is through physical fatigue, emotional turmoil or spiritual apathy - often all three!

I am not saying that we should avoid situations where we are exposed to these kinds of stresses - most missionary and ministry situations are stressful. Rather that when we are experiencing stresses that are overloading us, we need to recognise our need to make some changes, and not ignore them.

It is *not* failure to seek to maintain your well-being so that you can serve Christ to the best of your ability. How often have we heard it said of someone, "they should have left a long time ago," because it is recognised that they are no longer functioning as effective witnesses of Christ. It *is* failure when we continue on in a ministry when we no longer have the ability, physically, emotionally or spiritually, to cope with the demands of that ministry; when we do not recognise the extent of our own brokenness and the need to rebuild and recharge. It will show through in our relationships with those around us. Frustration, anger or withdrawal are likely symptoms.

The question then comes, what if my organisation does not have any ability to help or relieve me? Now we can easily start to take on board a responsibility that is not ours to own. Firstly we need to be honest and put our hand up so they know what we are experiencing. But then it is the responsibility of the organisation to find solutions, working with you. You don't need the added stress of taking on your manager's or organisation's responsibility to you. While I wish I could say that Christian missions and organisations should be able to identify encroaching symptoms of burnout in members and provide support to nip it in the bud, unfortunately some are not there yet. Thankfully it is a journey that many are now engaging in more seriously.

I was thankful that MAF senior management initially gave me a time frame to relieve me of duties, then engaged a psychologist who was able to give me counsel and a diagnosis for what I was experiencing. Unfortunately it came late in the day for me. Then, when I could no longer cope and needed to withdraw earlier than hoped, they continued to maintain us on an allowance for some months to facilitate recovery. This allowed me the opportunity to start a process of restoration and healing.

As I look back on my own story I recognise that I was not able to offer the support that many of my staff needed as they faced the impact of their stressors. My own experience and growing lack of confidence was blinding me in many ways to see others needs.

One of the unfortunate aspects of burnout and PTSD is that you don't recover fully from them. Like grief, we need to learn to incorporate them into our life as we work towards restoration and healing. We lose something of our former self, self-confidence often being a significant casualty. So in the restoration process, one of seeking to get back to who we want to be, we should now be aware of the red flags that we ignored or missed before. They now need to be incorporated into our new life so that we regain our self-confidence but hold it in tandem with a caution that stops us returning to the past.

I believe that it is in the brokenness and vulnerability that we have experienced that a greater ministry opens up for us, a greater opportunity for God to use us. We have discovered the reality of being clay jars, easily broken, with a new understanding that God's grace is sufficient for us; that God's power is made perfect in our weakness (2 Corinthians 12:9).

If this is your story too, then I pray you will find restoration and healing in body and mind, and fullness again in your spiritual walk with Christ.

'Waiting for Good News'
(from original watercolour)

Other books by Mike Jelliffe, published by Nenge Books:

- **The People of the Bird** (Nenge Series one). A novel set in PNG.*
- **The Power of the Bird** (Nenge Series two).*
- **Leading to Empower** - Biblical Perspectives on the Art of Leading and Managing People.*
- **The Cross** - The Wisdom and Power of God [**Diwai Kros** - Save na Strong Bilong Bikpela] (Inductive Bible Study in 1 Corinthians in English and Tok Pisin).
- **Turning the World Upside Down** - The Kingdom of God in Matthew's Gospel (Inductive Bible Study).

* Available as paperback and ebook through normal outlets.

These and other publications by Nenge Books are available for sale on www.nengebooks.com.

The video *Above & Beyond* can be obtained in electronic format by request, email to nengebooks1@gmail.com.

Please email feedback on this book to the author at nengebooks1@gmail.com.

www.ingramcontent.com/pod-product-compliance
Lightning Source LLC
Chambersburg PA
CBHW051435290426
44109CB00016B/1560